A Nighttime Guide to Paris

A NIGHTTIME GUIDE TO PARIS

By Jacques-Louis Delpal

LONDON HOUSE & MAXWELL
Elmsford   New York

Copyright by The British Book Centre, publishers of London House & Maxwell books and a division of Maxwell Scientific International, Inc.

All rights reserved.
Library of Congress Catalog Card No. 70-111891
SBN 8277-0342-2

Translated by Marianne Selengut, and updated from the most recent editions of *Ultra-Guide/Paris la Nuit*, published in Paris by Gouraud Editeur.

Printed in U.S.A.

TABLE OF CONTENTS

INTRODUCTIONS AND CONCLUSIONS   1
History and Geography   1
Attire   7
The Budget   10
The Calendar   11

CAFES AND BARS   13
Rive Gauche (Left Bank)   13
Rive Droite (Right Bank)   17

RESTAURANTS   23
Concorde/Etoile/les Ternes   25
Clichy/Pigalle/Montmartre   31
Palais-Royal/le Marais   35
Les Halles   37
Ile Saint-Louis/Ile de la Cite   39
Saint-Germain-des-Pres/Montparnasse   40
Saint-Michel/Mouffetard   49

CLUBS ET DISCOTHEQUES   53
Rive Gauche (Left Bank)   57
Rive Droite (Right Bank)   64

RATED "X"	69
The Debutantes	71
The Professionals	73
Between Boys	76
Neo-Women	79
Woman to Woman	82
CABARETS	85
Cabaret Girls	88
Strip-Tease Joints	94
"Specialized" Cabarets	98
Shows and Revues	101
Exotic Cabarets	103
MOSTLY MUSICAL	113
Supper Clubs	113
"Left Bank" Cabarets	117
Jazz Joints	120
SHOPPING AND OTHER PRACTICAL INFORMATION	123
The "Drugstores"	123
Shopping	128
Practical Information	130
APPENDICES	133
Other Nocturnal Distractions	133
The "Private" Nights	135
Who's Who in Night Life	137
Dictionary	142

Foreword

An obsessive night owl, Jacques-Louis Delpal has conscientious insomnia: two months after the publication of his "Paris la Nuit", which he had handed in to us in the spring of 1968, he brought us a new 1969 edition (the third within one trimester). The fundamental elements of life after midnight had not changed, but we could hardly refuse our author an official acknowledgment of the newly opened *La Goulue, l'Hôtel* and *le Bibelot*, and the reborn *Club Saint-Germain*. Neither could we refuse to salute the inauguration of *les Coulisses* and *la 5e avenue* . . .

This guide to insomniac Paris may seem subjective to the professionals and night lovers but even they could not deny that it is an honest one. Jacques-Louis Delpal did collect addresses, but he wanted to attempt more: conjecturing that life after midnight cannot be defined only in terms of stars, roosters, or forks, he offers us a real exposé of night-life and night people. Do forgive him if he stresses call-girls more than bars and if prices have changed during the printing of this book, which is much more than a mere directory. The author's main weakness is a weakness for the night.

THE EDITORS

INTRODUCTION AND CONCLUSION

History and Geography

All night-owls sight midnight on the belfry, but Parisian insomniacs know that every eight or ten years the bell tolls for local nocturnal doings. Without unsettling those meritorious day workers who, after turning off their TV's, go straight from slippers to sleep, obscure geological vibrations regularly upset the geography of Paris by night. This complicates the task of guide-book writers, and causes club owners and eminent alcoholics to moan together that "things have changed," suddenly realizing that a decade has slipped by.

The elders of the golden era of night life did not have to wait for *le Caroll's* closing to understand that they would never again see the violins of *Monseigneur,* and *Casanova,* the worldly jazz of *le Florence* and the very formal Fridays at *l'Elephant Blanc.* Unfortunately, nocturnal experience is fickle, and the night owls who jumped on the bandwagon of the first discotheques, and even the twisters of 1960, are quite disappointed today. They realize they are out of their depth in the contemporary night. The night they thought was theirs forever has dropped them like a courtesan abandoning a client who thought he would be loved always.

Maybe one day club, cabaret, bar and restaurant owners might ask an IBM computer to uncover the secret equation of night life: to explain why cycles that start with a bang in certain neighborhoods end in total neglect. For the moment, the insomnia exploiters are no more informed than their clients. They moaned in 1966 when business dropped off and cried somewhat in 1967. Then they either made some changes or resigned themselves to having known better times, now lost forever.

Night-owls who made the scene at the opening of *le Saint Hilaire* on rue Ponthieu or of the *New Jimmy's* aren't at the stage of the Montparnos (residents of Montparnasse) ripe for Ris-Orangis, who remember *le Dome* of their twenties over curry at *la Coupole*. But these night-owls are almost as square as the old Paroissiens who dream of the warmth of *le Lorientais*, the conversations at *le Nuage* and the elections of Miss Poubelle, while drinking bad coffee at *le Flore*. Régine, Castel, François-Patrice, Albert Minski and Paul Pacini, are still around to make their loyal clientele believe that night life is an eternal rebirth and that one dawn is just like the other. But insomniacs returning from a three-year voyage, need a guide and some good advice to find their way in the present night. Be it night-clubs or cabarets!

Geographically speaking, an unending migration to Saint-Germain-des-Prés and to a certain extent to Montparnasse has drained the right bank considerably. *Le Lido, le Moulin Rouge, le Crazy-Horse, Raspoutine, le Harry's Bar, l'Elysée-Matignon, le Club de l'Etoile* and *la Calvados* are only monuments towering above the flood, while everything else is submerged. Establishments with sparse satellites in a dead environment.

Pigalle is now only a forgotten song, neon lights blinking in the desert and a sad Saturday night faun. *Le Moulin Rouge* attracts a full house with its super-frous-frous and acquatic ballet, *le Cloche d'Or* still welcomes show-business people from Johnny Halliday to Raymond Devos, but they are mini-enclaves in a neighborhood where new permanent strip joints, charging 2.50F cover charge (plus drinks), form a pathetic row on the boulevard.

The "quartier" destroyed itself by dint of interest cups, payoffs, tastelessness and lack of imagination. At the *Folies-*

Pigalle, Mme Martini's efforts left their mark, *Eve* is still honest, *Sheherazade* continues to display its amazing oriental-rococco decor and an incredible old cymbal player, Maslova, is as rapturous as ever in the midst of the transvestites of *Madame Arthur.* And that's just too bad for the poor tourists who arrive by the bus load to the heart of rascally Paris to take in three cabarets for 90 or 100 francs, the members of a group on a spree having the advantage of being bored without being fleeced too much.

On the Champs-Elysées, the situation is different but still not good, despite the opening of the frenzied and comfortable *Psychedelic* just a few months after the inauguration of the now closed *Play Boy,* which had taken over the quarters of the old *Licorne:* after 11 p.m. the neighborhood is lifeless. Two or three years ago the district fell ill and it cannot get back on its feet, bringing luck now to drugstores and amazones only, the latter keeping up payments on the car thanks to obliging hitch-hikers. The departure of François-Patrice from rue Ponthieu symbolized the decay of the Champs, abandoned by a clientele that would rather play gin-rummy at home or park their cars for good at Saint-Germain-des-Prés. The days you went from "tambourés" at *le Saint-Hilaire* to the hully gully at *l'Etoile* and ended the night at *la Caravelle* or *la Calvados* are now gone. The Bernard Buffets, the Barclays, the Vadims, rich Lebanese, mundane dentists and the doubtful classes of playboys and cuties stay home or cross the Seine.

The area of the XVIe arrondissement (precinct) and Neuilly, where great night-owls hide from daylight, harbors only two or three discotheques. The presence of grand hotels and the myth of the Champs feeds only *le Lido, le Crazy Horse, le Sexy,* various less important carbarets and *la Calvados*—where ladies in mink and bleached hair come in at dawn, on the arms of graying gentlemen, for a light snack.

This is very little for the world's most beautiful avenue and its satellite streets. If we took away *le Lido* (which is about to expand) and *le Crazy Horse* (has already expanded) night life on the Champs-Elysées would be strictly confidential. To those who knew the *Carrousel* of the 1948-50's, *Carroll's, la Licorne,* and *le Saint Hilaire,* this situation looks ridiculous. The only reason for this downfall, besides the rush to Saint-Germain-des-Prés, is the gloominess of the Champs when the lights are out, despite the *Drug, Mini,* and *New Stores* and the vast spread of the neighborhood.

Today's night-owls are losing interest in the car, but they also don't like to cross the Champs-Elysées's no-man's-land back and forth, when they do the rounds of the clubs. At Saint-Germain they can stroll from rue St.-Benoit to rue Princesse or rue de l'Echaudé, but they need wheels to proceed from *l'Elysee Club* to *la Villa d'Este,* from *le Crazy* to *l'Etoile.* And they find it a bothersome task . . .

The resounding collapse of *Le Carnal* and *le Saint-Hilaire #1* did not discourage night promoters, judging by the new night spots opening in the neighborhood, but clearly, the Champs-Elysées will not be revived as a whole for 2 or 3 years. Saint-Germain first has to grow out of proportion and eventually overflow.

Saint-Germain is no longer the village of Gréco, Sartre, Luter, Gélin and Annabelle, it is a large borough grown rich overnight and developing much like Saint Tropez. *Lipp* alone did not change, it still is the bistro evoked by Léon-Paul Fargue in *Le Piéton de Paris.* Roger Cazes posts in front of his revolving doors "90 minute wait" and has his habitués wait for fifteen minutes.

When the Paroissiens of yesteryear aren't ruminating memories over a plate of herrings from the Baltic, they take up quarters at *le Flore* sometimes at *les Deux Magots.* Since the advent of the rock, long hair and "minets" (see dictionary in back), rue Saint-Benoît belongs to the singer, musicians and different varieties of "yé-yé" (hipsters)—on the sidewalk of *le Bilboquet,* the other side being shared by students and tourists.

For a long time, Saint-Germain had been confined to 100 meters of boulevard, the cross-road and rue Saint-Benoît, but these borders proved to be flexible, as newcomers who wanted to take advantage of the "germano-pratin" label settled there. Since the naming of boroughs isn't under control, the Odéon can escape the less prestigious Quartier Latin to become part of the "Greater-Saint-Germain-des-Prés."

Introduction and Conclusion

It is now exceedingly difficult to park in this quartier, even if you are willing to risk getting a parking ticket—generously distributed—but crowds will attract crowds. The very costly installation of *le Drugstore* marked the transition from the Saint-Germain-des-Prés of buddies and August night-owls to a Saint-Germain open to all, the No. 1 district of nighttime Paris, where onlookers, tourists and young commandos from the suburbs, the middle class on a spree, artists and old-timers meet and jostle each other but don't necessarily mix.

Saint-Germain-des-Prés, once a village for intellectual bohemians, is now one of the most financially successful areas encompassing *le King, Lipp, Castel, le Bilboquet* and dozens of all-night spots. It is an immense leisure factory where millions are spent for decoration. Every fortnight marks the opening of a new gadget store, night club or restaurant. The tide continues to rise, dragging a lot of money along, foreboding spectacular bankruptcies the day Saint-Germain's luck runs out.

After one a.m. you can stroll on the quiet Boul'Mich: students who don't have exams the next day prefer to walk along the Contrescarpe, pleasantly revitalised by beatnicks, hippies and the clients of some restaurants. The only section of town besides Saint-Germain-des-Prés where they go to bed really late is Montparnasse. François Patrice recently joined Régine there. There too you can find cabarets, still alive and well.

Very limited in space, the little island of night life consisting of rue Bréa and rue Vavin, profits from the insolvency of Pigalle: *Elle et Lui, le Carrousel, la Villa, le Kit-Kat, le O.K. Bar et le Smart*—cabarets and night bar-restaurants—attract a clientele that might not be welcome in the discotheques yet keeps late hours and loves Champagne.

A strange world of strip-teasers, lesbians, transvestites, hostesses stays up till dawn. Montparnasse has been progressing in inverse proportions to Pigalle, because the streets are cleaner, because the two main club owners in the neighborhood do not pay off taxi drivers and because at least one-half of the clientele consists of habitués. There you can petition a lady on the street without worrying about her tanned protector lurking in the shadows; there you can watch the show over a drink, and not spend a fortune.

Cashiers, barmen, wardrobe attendants—sociologists of night life—state that the geographical change that occurred in nighttime Paris, the success of the left bank at the expense of the right bank, is coupled with an evolution in the clientele:

★ It is younger. A new wave of minets and mini-jerkeuses ('teeny-boppers') obsessed with dance more than with sex or alcohol, have relegated discotheque haunters to wallflower benches where they bitterly drink and regret that they did not have the presence of mind to evolve from the twist.

Junior night-owls now shy off the sordid *Palladium* and the atmosphere at *la Cage*. But they pile up in the basement of *le Bilboquet* and still visit *le Club de la Rousse* while dreaming of *Castel*.

★ It goes to bed earlier. The night-owls who used to close nightclubs at dawn now accept late morning business appointments. The swinging discotheques, crowded from midnight to two, empty out before 3 a.m.

★ It has lost its ambulatory urge. Clients who could easily "make" three or four clubs a night, no longer have the courage to hop in and out of their car for a change of whiskey and barman.

★ The "locomotives" (fast set) have either disappeared or have decided to disappear properly; the gangs split up and night-leaders became estranged from their following because of such outside interests as week-ending, the country home, a taste of travel and winter sports—even work. Eddie Barclay, Sacha Distel, and Vadim have been checking their night outings, and the chum-habitués of discotheques got tired of waiting with a bottle of scotch for the birth of a new dawn. Night time professionals sadly had to realize that Parisians increasingly prefer dining at home and manifest a perverse liking for Gin-rummy, poker and even gadget games.

★ Going out less regularly, night-owls are losing their former habits and no longer feel obligated to sit in the same place at the same club every time they spend the evening out. Only two or three years ago they moved in a closed circuit, but now they are willing to mix with anonymous nightclubbers, formerly considered "out". They sample . . .

★ Beyond a certain age and income, the night clientele is regaining an interest in supper clubs, which were faring quite badly in the days of the twist. Executives, industrialists, doctors and businessmen will spend 50 to 150 francs per person for conventional though often copious programs. Many are returning to Russian cabarets, where Gypsies and Russian emigrants have once again struck up their violins and balalaikas.

Introduction and Conclusion

It took six years to change from the twist to the jerk, from the right to the left bank, from immutable flock-outings to forays with a date or a friend; but these changes in night behavior were crystallized in a span of time starting in summer 1967 and ending in late winter 1968. While becoming parsimonious with their insomnia and even with their money, they started to care about comfort, the decor, and even opportunities to eat well. The days when an entertainer who was on a first-name basis with Tout-Paris could seat his audience on bad stools in some smoky cave, following a grilled meat and herbs supper at a better "gargotte" (tavern) are definitely gone.

The King Club was first to install air conditioning, Dunlapillo and velvet pile carpeting, replaced at the slightest snag. Then Leila followed with her luxuriously comfortable *Ruby's*. Following the trend, the brothers Minski revitalised their discotheque by adding two fancy restaurants, an aquarium-bar and a billiard room, while François-Patrice was tearing down the former *Eléphant Blanc* to create his new *Saint-Hilaire* with several levels and balconies under a night restaurant.

A new cycle has recently begun. Financial amateurism, the "buddy-above-all" style and tinkering are outmoded. The new kings of the night are making improvements in order to hold on to the complex night-owls who now want to spend their nights in nocturnal complexes; the American way. Life after midnight is creating a paradox: salesmen of darkness and neon lights, are democratizing night-life at the cost of extravagant rates; doors open more and more liberally and prices climb higher and higher.

Attire

Money and fame open all doors to night-life, regardless of dress, but the amateur night-owl must fit his wardrobe to the taste of doormen or usherettes who watch newcomers at the entrance. As long as you are not considered a good client or a habitué, a passion for polo shirts, open collars, or blazers could jeopardize your admittance to a night club where only friends can dress casually.

Mini-gowns and smoking jackets turned everything upside down, and hippy outfits became a source of confusion to night cognocenti, except in certain cabarets where the tie or the polka-dot bow still symbolizes nocturnal class. It is hard to bar Claudine Auger's entrance to a gala because she is wearing a paper dress and it is impossible to make President Rosko and Johnny Hallyday see that a dressy cat-or dromedary-hide suit is not proper attire . . .

After all is said and done, you have to be somebody or know someone who is in order to have them consider your Lap hunting suit a tuxedo. This author suffered many a scolding for forgetting his tie, and he knows he had to compromise in his clothing before they would complement him os the finish of his jeans and the silkiness of his turtle-necks. To those of his readers who are beginners, he suggests accepting that in night-life there is one law for the rich and another for the poor. So dress properly at the start hoping that you will yet walk through Parisian nights with pelt on your back and psychedelic tatoos on your face.

Clothiers, who have invaded today's discotheques en masse will be only too glad to advise you. They will tell you that synthetic fabrics have the advantage of not creasing much on humid nights, but they nevertheless are not to be recommended. Their textures don't appeal to caressing hands of snobbish little girls and neither will they bear the faintest contact with cigarettes without fatal results. "Alpaga" is your best bet; it creases madly behind the knees and in the back, but it compensates with light-weight (it makes up to a certain extent for the whims of Parisian air-conditioning, one of the world's worst).

Lightly dressed, the night-owl will first wear a black or anthracite blue suit, an all-weather outfit that will insure him quiet anonymity at Régine's and give him a distinguished air in cabarets. We don't advise the sinister blue of the somewhat stiff trade people, but we approve of light colors for first acquaintance with the night. They contrast with the dark uniformity of men who dress to go out.

Introduction and Conclusion 9

At the second stage, the signature of Cardin, the Renoma brothers, Ted Lapidus, or Mayfair permits realization of every fantasy, if you haven't already developed expensive habits at André Bardot's or any of his friends from "le Groupe des Cinq." When you pay them regular visits to keep up with the fashion, you may become familiar enough with discotheque doorkeepers to retort with "do you know where this is from?" when they gently take you to task for wearing a vest-suit that resembles the garb of roadworkers or an army on the run.

Beyond the stage of the Mao-suit, the Lenin-collar and the zippered jacket, you can indulge in anything, including a tailored copy of the garb worn by the "clochards" (Parisian bums) who mount guard in front of *Castel* and *le King Club*. As a matter of fact it is imperative that a young singer on his way to fame bundle up in every shred of cloth he can find, borrow, or buy.

Time and again, a club owner determined to shut his half-open door will say that the cowl makes the monk. Driving back all the anonymous polos, he may say to a habitué "you must give me your Nepalese shirt, I just adore it . . . but it does bother me a little that you are not wearing a tie. I just threw out some twenty persons who were improperly dressed!"

On Friday nights you answer that you are already dressed for the weekend. On Sunday, and even Monday, you assure him that you are just back from the week-end. Tuesdays you pretend that it is your night out with the boys; Wednesdays, for want of a better excuse, your surly retort is that you already made the rounds of the clubs, and they accepted you everywhere without problems. Saturday nights you won't be dressed any worse than the crowd that regularly invades the most restricted clubs.

It will always be essential that your untidiness look thought out and therefore elegant. However, nothing should stop you from noting that a sober suit or a tuxedo is no more embarrassing than shepherd's rags. As to your date, she does as she wishes: putting her long gown aside for galas (incompatible with the "jerk" and low stools), she knows that a perfect body looks good in anything. Do suggest, however, that she wear pantihose or tights if her hemline borders her waist and ask her not to move too abruptly if she decided to let the steel or leather shells of her last Paco Rabanne hang over her naked breasts. Forbid her to wear a "petite laine" (shawl) on her shoulders. It is not prohibited in discotheques and does very well in cabarets, but we hate it.

The Budget

The Parisian night is not the most expensive one in the world, but insomnia may become a luxury. According to some favorite itineraries, here are a few sample budgets for a couple.

★ *A sensible night at Saint-Germain-des-Prés:*
Supper at *Lipp's,* a drink at *Castel's,* sundry expenses (cigarets, wardrobe, tips): 150 francs.

★ *A tour of the discotheques:*
Multiply the number of stops by 40 francs, whether you stop at *l'Etoile, chez Castel,* at *le King* or *chez Régine.* If you want to linger in a club, and you are thirsty, order a bottle (180 to 200 francs): you can finish it another time, if you don't drain it.

★ *A sedate Russian night:*
Dinner at *Kortchma,* a drink at *Sheherazade:* 120 francs.

★ *A mad Russian night:*
Champagne dinner at *Raspoutine,* a drink at *le Tzarevitch:* a total of 500 francs if you don't fling yourself at the caviar. Prepare, in addition, generous tips for the gypsies who play "Dark eyes" at your request.

★ *An unusual night in Montparnasse:*
Dinner at *la Coupole* or at *Saint-Vincent,* half an hour at *Carrousel,* a drink at *Elle et Lui, la Dolce Vita* or *le Kit-Kat,* spaghetti at dawn at *the Saint-Hilaire:* count on 250 francs if you don't overdo it and if you don't introduce a "garçonne" (lesbian in male role) or a transvestite to your wife.

★ *A classical and expensive night:*
A show-supper at *la Tête de l'Art,* a drink in a discotheque. About 400 F.

★ *A night in Pigalle:*
Dinner at *la Cloche d'Or,* a drink at *Folies-Pigalle,* a drink at *Madame Arthur:* estimate 200 francs.

Introduction and Conclusion 11

★ *A reasonably priced night on the left bank:*
Punch at *la Rhunerie Martiniquaise,* dinner at *Vagenende,* a drink at *l'Ecluse* or at *le Cheval d'Or:* about 90 francs.

★ *With a couple of foreign friends (4 persons):*
—Apéritifs at *le Fouquet's,* dinner at *le Lido,* a drink *chez Raspoutine:* roughly 500 francs (cloakroom and tip included).
—Dinner at *le King Club,* refreshments at *le Crazy Horse,* a drink at *la Calvados.* About 450 francs.

The Calendar

One night doesn't resemble any other. The rules of the evening are seasonal. The atmosphere in clubs changes considerably from day to day, from month to month.

★ Monday, Tuesday, Wednesday are usually calm days. The clientele has class. These are the habitués, too eminent to rise early on weekdays.

★ Thursday is lively but well-dressed. The evening belongs to night rovers who come in before the end-of-the-week-crowd and leave Paris for the week-end.

★ Friday has become the rich-man's Saturday. This "soirée" is being spoiled by the growing five-day business week, but financial returns are good.

★ Saturday, the real night-owls abandon the night for the country, or try to cheat their friends at poker on home grounds. The democratic pressure of the masses is such that the doors of the most intransigent clubs give way, for the greater good of the cash-box.

★ On national and religious holiday eves, the Saturday clientele frolics. Avoid the clubs if you like the night.

★ Christmas makes the night-owl melancholy. He dreams of his childhood pine-tree, or sadly contemplates the fate of the legitimate or illegitimate children he squandered between the *Crazy* and *Castel.*

★ New Year's Eve there is unlimited noise and unrestricted kissing. Prices rise, it is crowded and deadly.

★ August 15 is the day Parisians who are held back by their jobs in the most beautiful city in the world scoff at those leisure-crazy citizens who foolishly tarry in Saint-Topez, Cannes or Biarritz. Sometimes they improvise festivities while dreaming of the arial bridge from Paris to Nice. Hotel-work has always been subject to seasonal fluctuations. Night life too is sensitive to falling leaves as well as to the first snowfall and blossoming buds.

★ The return in September is slow but promising. Night club owners lose their tan while building castles in Spain. Journalists, specializing in night-life try to guess which will be the haunts of nocturnal Tout-Paris (jet-set). From le Salon de l'Auto to Goncourt, clubs take off steadily, while cabarets enjoy full houses. Everybody is happy.

★ Before the end-of-year festivities, night-professionals dig up last year's garlands. They admit they are undergoing a low phase but already dream of the profits from the "Saint-Sylvestre"

★ In January, "animateurs" (major-domos), cabaret-owners and barmen together, sing the sorrowful stanzas of "it's worse than last year," the melancholy song that will live as long as the night. What causes these lamentations: gastronomic and financial excesses during the holiday season, a general low in the country, and an exodus to winter resorts (moderate off-season prices).

★ In February, the melancholy turns into depression: taxes, bad weather, Courchevel (winter resort)....

★ In March, despite the abortive attempts to distract the client who broke a leg at Courchevel, the owners begin to take heart once again and virtually light up by April.

★ In May and June, a flow of tourists who are no longer afraid of de Gaulle's bite, make the scene. Good season for cabarets. Clubs on the other hand see their clientele file out without warning: time for the Festival de Cannes, first stay in the deserted but divine Saint-Tropez.

★ In July, cabaret owners cheer and the discotheque owners whine: snapped up by the sun, night-club haunters now crash the spots on the Côte d'Azur.

★ In August, Parisians watch for the opening of *Lipp,* call themselves "aoûtiens" and turn Saint-Germain-des-Prés into a night ghetto. Foreigners who are deprived of the joy of sitting at a table on rue Saint-Benoît, retreat to the humdrum cabarets. Nothing is less monotonous than the Parisian night: it is always worse off than the eve, the month, or the year before, they say. Yet it isn't doing that badly....

Cafes and Bars

Neon lights of Parisian "bistrots" (pubs) reflect on plastic coated walls till two in the morning and sometimes until a wan union with the rising sun, but Paris lacks bars for greeters of the dawn.

If you are tired of rendez-vous at *le Flore, les Deux-Magots, le Bilboquet,* at *Paris, l'Ascot* or the neighborhood café, join your nocturnal partner at a restaurant or in a club after 11:30. Except for the famous *Harry's, le Bougnat, le Village* and *le Smart* (not to mention the girlie-bars on Pigalle, or the daytime bar at the Ritz.) it seems that the life of scotch-without-jerk stops at 10 or 11 p.m.

Rather than give you dozens of addresses of joints where barmen yawn as 10 o'clock rolls by, we will limit our listing to several pleasant or at least "possible" bars. The title and the style which we are trying to give this book prevent us from the numerous nocturnal stops we have made, which led us to despair of night bars. This very limited chapter will be strictly subjective—with your kind indulgence.

"Rive Gauche" (Left Bank)

Le Bar Bac. 13, rue du Bac, 548-06-07.
Has a clientele of writers—their local hangout—but its hours are somewhat whimsical: it can close at midnight or 5 a.m.

Le Bar Basque. 10, rue Delambre, 326-67-77.
Is practically empty at dinner-time but fills up around midnight and stays open till daybreak. A rustic decor, a pleasant night

menu, dishes native to the Landes region and amiable service. Estimate 20 to 25 francs for a norturnal meal. (Closed on Sunday)

Le Bar Vert. 14, rue Jacob, 326-83-07.
Sometimes receives Scandinavian clients, whose fairness contrasts with the tan of habitués from the land of the sun. They don't "jerk" much on the narrow dance-floor of this little bar (open until 3 a.m.), but the cha-cha and the merengue are danced with West-Indian agility. Calm and smiling, the clients of *le Bar Vert* chat or play 421 without giving a second thought to the non-existing décor. (Closed on Monday)

Le Bougnat. 15, rue Séguier, 033-31-55.
Stays open till 3 in the morning. It resembles a little *le Nuage* of 10 years ago, though less "literary" and more comfortable.

You can dine or sup at *le Bougnat,* but most of the clients just have a scotch (12 francs at the table). Jean, who opened the place in 1963, on the premises of a real "bougnat" (retail coal shop), bought the tables and chairs at the Marché aux Puces (flea-market) and matched his lighting to the classical music quietly diffused throughout the room.

The clientele consists of journalists, comedians, singers and rugby players. On certain nights, Enrico Macias, Pierre Perret and Laurent Terzieff rub elbows with a group of stocky players from the XV de France team. Admission is private club-style: better be accompanied by a habitué.

Les Deux-Magots. 170, boulevard Saint-Germain, 548-55-25.
Offers a strategic terrace to whomever can find a table. If you manage to sit near the entrance you can watch the comings and goings on the square, arrivals at *Lipp,* motorized friends stopping for a red light, and paper buyers at the "kiosque". It is a perfect spot for young people who know everybody in the neighborhood, and on sunny days it is a rather pleasant place for tourists.

The peaceful newspaper readers in the room would be very surprised if Alfred Jarry were to be resurrected. In the days this famous café was merely an ale-house, he had shot a few rounds at the ceiling for fun. A pair of buddhas, standing there since 1870, had been spared. They lazily watch over an anonymous clientele the way they watched over Léautaud, André Breton, Jean Gireaudoux and the post-liberation readers of *Combat.*

Le Flore. 172, boulevard Saint Germain, 548-55-26.
Had been adopted by Sartre and Simone de Beauvoir during the

cold nights of the occupation. Mr. Boubal had the good taste to heat the place. Before the war, l'Action Française—headed by Maurras and Barrés—held sessions there (often enough to inspire *Au Signe de Flore*), which didn't bother the gauche young intellectuals of the "Groupe Octobre," enlivened by les Frères Prévert, Marcel Duhamel and an unknown singer named Mouloudji.

Camus had been at *le Flore,* Sartre and Simone de Beauvoir were finally driven away by a hoard of long-haired "existentialists" who could hardly decode *l'Etre et le Néant* (Being and Nothingness) even if they consulted Lalande. Roger Vailland, and Sartre's secretary Jean Cau were to hold out longer. But not as long as the tourists who now keep watch on the terrace, hoping to meet some ghost from the Grand-Saint-Germain-des-Prés.

These phantoms, who feel lost among the "New Wave" roaming rue Saint-Benoît in fitted uniforms and show-biz-casuals, still return to this "café de sous-prefecture" (André Billy) which is too important for even a lowly civil servant to come in regularly for a game of "manille" (cards). They prefer the imitation-leather on the ground floor to the plaid covered first floor (2nd floor in America). The young people who take good care of their Colonel, are far too pleased with Mr. Boubal's old apartment to let anything interrupt their melodic chatter.

The London Tavern. 3, rue du Sabot, 548-42-39.
Was inaugurated on January 31, 1968, by Winston Churchill, Jr., and the ambassador from Great Britain. Welcomed by two (fake) bobbies, a (real) British doorman and a small artificial smog cloud, they saw that the misadventures of the Concorde and the mishaps of the travailistes didn't in any way affect the anglomania of the Left Bank.

Robert Probst, creator of the *Winston Churchill,* keeps looking to England and dreams of transforming rue du Sabot into a "mini-street." For a start, he hoisted the Union Jack over an old three-story house that Slavik dismantled in order to combine it with pieces of an old pub brought over from some suburb of London. It has a rectangular bar on the ground floor, an Indian-army style bar on the first and a whiskey palace on the second. You can have supper there at hours when London pubs are closed. It isn't expensive in a neighborhood where the prices keep climbing. Open until 2 a.m.

Le Nuage. 5, rue Bernard-Palissy, 222-56-25.
Has a lovely Germano-pratin (pertaining to Saint-Germain-des-Prés) past. But things no longer happen there, the place is dark, clients linger till very late chatting against a reserved musical

background. The neighborhood's old-timers, some of whom have migrated to the right bank, occasionally reappear.

La Pergola. 1, rue du Four, 033-59-10.
Had disappeared for a long time behind a construction barrier, but reopened and found a wiser clientele. Whiskey is 6 francs and beer is 2.50; you can dine late and well on the first floor for roughly 20 to 25 francs.

La Rhumerie Martiniquaise. 166, boulevard Saint-Germain, 033-28-94.
In the summer, its terrace is the most sought-after place in the neighborhood. The friendliness, ease and relaxed pace of the service, the perfume, the flavor and the tonic of the punches create a tropical illusion. There you can see a variety of pretty girls, watch the comings and goings on the "carrefour (intersection) Mabillion," linger on without having to reorder too often, all this till two thirty in the morning.

Le Rosebud. 11 bis, rue Delambre, 326-95-28.
Is a night bar frequented by the compatriots of Citizen Kane, Italians and Montparnos of all nationalities including French. Modern jazz records, minimum lighting, calm customers, scotch at 8.50 francs. You can quiet your pangs of hunger with "tartare" (minced steak meat w. sauce) or hamburgers for 12 francs, until 5 or 6 a.m.

Le Smart. 3, rue Bréa, 326-72-99.
Is kept by an old hand in night life: Jean-Jacques has 16 years of experience at Montparnasse. It is a toned-down bar rather than a restaurant, yet when 5 a.m. rolls by, the habitués of nearby cabarets, club entertainers and personnel often ask the boss "what is there to eat?" For 20 or 25 francs, or less if you can make do with a "gratinée" cheese dish or a pair of frankfurters, you can have a pleasant meal at dawn. For 6 francs, you can have one "for the road." (Closed on Sunday)

Le Temps Perdu. 54, rue de Seine, 326-73-56.
Offers a quiet clientele, a reasonable rosé, beer and whiskey until 2 in the morning. This quiet night bar, managed by a debonair barman, amateur of P.M.U. (horse-betting), took up quarters in a room abandoned by the vagabond Jean-Claude Merle. The decor is oldish and restful, the Irish coffee is scanty but honestly charged with whiskey imported from Dublin. (Closed on Tuesday).

Le Village. 7, rue Gozlin, 326-80-19.
Is part of the history of Saint-Germain-des-Prés, but the nights

are less wild and alcoholic now than during the "Belle Epoque" of the neighborhood. Writers, comedians, journalists are among the anonymous but steady clients. You can eat decently for some 20 francs.

Other places, possible or bearable.

—le Bonaparte. 42, rue Bonaparte, 326-42-81.
—Pub Castel. 15, rue Princess, 326-90-22.
(for night-club habitués, beer from the tap.)
—le Chai de l'Abbaye. 26, rue de Buci, 326-68-26.
(for amateurs of good wine at the counter; open all night)
—le Dôme. 108, bld Montparnasse, 033-53-61.
—le Falstaff. 42, rue du Montparnasse, 326-91-34.
(all night)
—le Mabillon. 164, bld. St.-Germain, 326-68-20.
—Old Navy. 150, bld St-Germain, 326-88-09.
—chez Popoff. 8, rue de la Huchette, 033-96-14.
(for beatnicks only)
—la Rotonde. 105, bld Montparnasse, 548-38-24.
—*see also* the drugstores and, in our chapter on restaurants, the establishments where you can stop for a drink.

Rive Droite (The Right Bank)

Le Bar Belge. 75, avenue de Saint-Ouen, 627-41-01.
The neighborhood is impossible, but if you love beer, you can make the sacrifice. *Le Bar Belge* is truly the uncontested temple to beer. They serve some thirty varieties. There you will discover that beer, like wine, is a noble drink. And sometimes highly alcoholic. Don't try to have too much during one evening. On your way out, you might be surprised to see that you cannot find your car or remember your own address. (Open until 1 a.m., closed on Monday.)

Le Bar du Bellman. 39, rue François—1er, 226-56-28.
Is tiny and decked in plaid, but you can wait for that model from Balmain in the adjoining hall while sipping a rosé or a scotch. Attractively thin women, journalists . . . and fluctuating closing-hours, that depend more on the clientele than on the barman. You could arrange to meet there before a late dinner, but on slow nights you may find the lights out at 11 p.m.

Le Bar du George V. 31, avenue George V, 225-35-22.
Delights those who crave cocktails and quiet, but it closes a bit too early for true night-owls. It would be very risky to meet your date there at 11 p.m.

Le Bar Romain. 6, rue Caumartin, 073-58-48.
Adjoins the Olympia: you must be "in show business" and very compressible if you wish to find a seat there after a grand Première or a "Musicorama."

Paul, barman for the past 20 years, was inspired by show business. He baptised his new blend of fruit-juices (for nice yé-yés) "Tube," then he made it alcoholic and named the new cocktail "Olympia." He offers all varieties of whiskey till 2 a.m. Mr. Papillon, the owner of *Bar Romain* got rid of the "Filles-de-la-Madeleine" but jealousy preserved the frescoes created in 1905 by a first-prize winner in le Prix de Rome who was obsessed by Petrone and Latin Dolce Vita. (We especially liked: the representation of Tiberius's supper in the den of S. Gallius and Messalina).

A man of many interests, M. Papillon catalogued the 1,200 automobile firms existing in France since 1900, but collecting key-holders is his main pursuit. It is he who coined the word "copocléophile." Despite an enviable guest book, opened for the first time by Lucienne Delyle, he doesn't rest on his laurels. He just undertook to enlarge his cellar in order to accommodate a little club for show business people and a small regular clientele.

Le Bar des Théatres. 6, avenue Montaigne, 359-34-88.
Has expanded successfully: calm and more sophisticated than before, it has kept its trade of actors, authors and dancers (le Studio, le Théâtre and la Comédie des Champs-Elysées are across the street). You may meet there models from neighboring maisons-de-couture (fashion houses) as well as show-biz people. Unpretentious menu (till 1:30 a.m.)

La Belle Ferronnière. 53, rue Pierre-Charron, 225-03-82.
Harbors till 9 p.m. neighborhood cover-girls and models. Friday evening, after having put the finishing touches to Paris-Match, journalists crowd the place till 1:30 a.m. (closing time.)

Café de la Paix. place de l'Opéra, 073-35-44.
There is no artist, star, or celebrity that has not at one time or another passed through its revolving doors, the first such in Paris. Nowadays one meets there only tourists, jewelers of place Vendôme and "les petits rats de l'Opéra" (junior ballet corp). The place is gigantic and aesthetically pleasing, but it

Cafés and Bars

is a little "passé". You can have a nice but costly supper there (till 1 a.m.).

Le Cintra. 6, square de l'Opéra—Louis Jouvet, 073-74-14.
Receives in its discotheque, "yé-yé"s (hipsters) from the nearby Olympia, but still serves Port to amateurs of muted conversation and refreshment. They serve supper too in this calm, sober and pleasant bar that stays open after theatres close. (Closed on Sunday)

Le Deauville. 75, Champs-Elysées, 225-08-64.
Is a café with excessively bright, clean and anonymous neon lights. You can stop for a drink there after the movies, at perfectly normal prices.

Le Donkey-Magali Club. 3, rue Chauveau-Lagarde, 265-34-05.
Was taken over late 1967 by singer Robert Ripa, his wife, now the cashier, and his son, their waiter. The three of them offer a wonderful meridional "famille Duraton" number to their guests, who usually come with very pretty girls. Between two songs and a guitar tune (he keeps it discreet), Robert Ripa claims that his chef can prepare any dish native to any country. You don't have to believe him, but you can eat well till dawn for approximately 35 francs.

Le Donkey is nonetheless a bar (drinks range from 6 to 10 francs). In the small underground discotheque a whiskey is 12 francs.

La Factorerie. 5, boulevard Malesherbes, 265-96-86.
Sometimes has customers who are disturbing in appearance only. Cheetahs have been seen playing lazily in the room, totally indifferent to the cocktail drinkers, who dream of faraway places till 2 in the morning.

We do not guarantee the presence of such felines, but you will find there insomniac monkeys and a weird atmosphere. This is highly rewarding in a neighborhood like Saint-Augustin, where everything is terribly dead at night-owl's breakfast hour. The spot is strange yet quite respectable. (Closed on Sunday)

Le Fouquet's. 99, Champs-Elysées, 359-59-54.
Is calm, and comfortable; the bar is open till 1:30 a.m. The tasteful silence maintained is never shattered, even when a moldo-valaque producer discusses film distribution with a specialist of cinéma-volapük. Martinis are served generously, service is discreet, and the house famous. On the whole it is an appropriate roosting place for peachful evening doves.

Le Harry's Bar. 5, rue Daunou, 073-73-00.
Is headed by Andy MacElhone who often stutters (but not when he says that his cocktails are "immobilizing"). As every "immobilized" gentlemen knows, Andy is the son of Harry MacElhone, who renamed the *"Sank Roo Donoo"* bar—*Harry's* half a century ago. He had taken over a business set up by Tod Sloan, the Yves Saint-Martin of that period.

Members of the International Bar-Flies club (amateurs of alcohol from every part of the world, who greet each other with a bzz-bzz and three taps on the back) are not the only ones who stay up till 4 in the morning, sometimes even later, to drink *Harry's* 50-odd whiskeys. Ever since Scott Fitzgerald and Hemingway, any young American author taking a trip to Europe, traditionally gets intoxicated on rue Daunou in the company of French colleagues and journalists. Boxing and Rugby fans too have a weakness for *Harry's*, its dark woodwork and university pennants. All this doesn't inconvenience Jeanne Moreau and Marguerite Duras in the slightest.

Bar haunters who address the owner with the familiar "tu," rarely go down to the basement where jazz and ragtime tunes are played on a piano. Within arm's reach of a bottle, they wait for the two longest nights on Harry's calendar: the night of the presidential elections in America, and December 31. New Year's Eve has the added attraction that you can kiss your pretty companion at midnight and 7 a.m. too, a second time, when midnight strikes in New York.

Le Pam-Pam. 73, Champs-Elysées, 259-67-83.
Has branches on place de l'Opéra, in Mexico and Conakry, which seems like internationalism of the best kind. You can drink whiskey till 1:30 a.m., eat at the bar or dine more comfortably in the basement. This entitles you to soft pianistics and a moderate check: 15 to 20 francs.

Le Plaza Athénée. at the corner of rue Montaigne and rue du Boccador, 359-85-23.
Entertains till 11 o'clock timid dusk rabbits at the quiet and pleasant British bar located in the basement. Confirmed insomniacs meet on the ground floor, open till 1:30 a.m. For 40 francs or more they can at least avoid looking for a restaurant by having supper right there.

Le Pub Winston Churchill. 5, rue de Presbourg, 553-75-35.
Was the first comfortable stronghold of triumphant anglomania. You can eat there (in British fashion of course) till 1:45 a.m., but you may sip one of the 60 whiskeys-maison at the bar till 3:30; later on Rugby fanatics exchange comments

there on the game's great matches. Among their whiskeys we highly recommend their Ballantine—30 years old with but one fault, its price: 22 francs—and the pure-malt "scotch." White like vodka, the Strathisla belongs to the great family of Chivas.

If a British breakfast, washed down with beer on tap does not satisfy you, you can top it off after libations with a delicious slice of salmon, a "bouillon de tortue" (turtle soup), tasty pies, or a couple of well-done sausages from Cambridge.

RESTAURANTS

The night isn't good council when it comes to gastronomic decisions. Night-owls recall the hesitation-waltz at midnight, when they don't know which direction to take. Except for a few obvious classics like *Lipp, la Cloche d'Or,* the restaurant at *Castel l'Elysée-Club,* a few anonymous *Jour et Nuits,* the attractive restaurant at *King* and the blue first floor of the *Saint-Hilaire,* chevroned insomniacs have a hard time finding a place to go to after the show. At 4 a.m. they still haven't decided where to find wide-awake oysters or a breakfast-fondue.

Like night-life, night-gastronomy is varied. If it is easy to classify establishments by neighborhood, it is much harder to couple restaurants where you can have supper with a lady and "bistrots" where you can forget the rising sun and your lack of sleep in beastly over-eating. It all depends on your mood, your appetite, your level of intoxication and the person you are with. If she doesn't fall into your arms, don't blame us: the hamburger and our advice may not necessarily be the cause.

To avoid any misunderstanding, we warn you now that *Laserre, le Grand Véfour, Jamin,* or *les Lyonnais,* are not today and never will be night restaurants. The personnel at *Lucas-Carton* occasionally does stay awake to welcome Claude François after a Première at the Olympia, but *Maxim's* is the only chic restaurant that goes on merrily past the stroke of midnight.

This generally doesn't alarm the obsessive night-prowler, who eats out of idleness, to please a famished beauty, or to forget one drink too many. His palate diverted by alcohol, and his senses more easily awakened by a girl from *Castel* than by a well-cooked hen, he grants only relative importance to what he finds in his plate. While giving 6 or 7,000 Parisian insomniacs addresses they all knew but quickly forgot, we wish to satisfy epicures who want to stray, fork in hand, through the night.

Immunized by the dog food served at *the Stardust,* and *la Cage,* we won't be poisoned by scullions who strongly protest that they were unfairly judged and unjustly forgotten. It is therefore with clear conscience that we have selected:

—Restaurants where you can have a late dinner or supper; where midnight cooking matches midday cooking; where you can entertain a novice in night-life. Places that have the good taste to compensate for their culinary deficiencies with mood or atmosphere. Places where the clientele is "prime" (in butcher's terms). Briefly, restaurants you won't leave with cramps or an "adieu" from your date.

—Spots for confirmed night-people, where the food is sometimes good, often passable and from time to time poor. Places that are rarely costly and where you can chat with a friend or buy a snack for a girl whom the wrong side of the night doesn't drive into a panic. A place where you recuperate before braving the first morning traffic jams.

Among these spots are well-known ones like *la Calavados,* calm ones like *la Caravelle,* or pleasant ones like *la Fringale.* Others may be sordid-looking, but try to overlook the shabbiness of early-morning bistrots by remembering that the night isn't young anymore. And forgive us for speculating that you could have ended up worse.

We close this prologue to a listing that is useful but incomplete, with a reminder that we have purposely skipped neighborhoods which are not frequented at night and that we have probably forgotten to mention a few charming spots (many a night place disappears prematurely if it doesn't readily change its cook, sign, or prices.)

Concorde/Etoile/Les Ternes

BEFORE 2 A.M.

Maxim's. 3, rue Royale, 265-27-94.
Is the only "big" one where the personnel bravely crosses midnight. But the days when some wild grandmother of a girl from *Castel* climbed on marquis de Nedonchel's (called pattefolle) or Feydeau's table, are gone. The fluffy elegance, the service and maybe the prices intimidate the discotheque generation—who by the way, never "learned to eat."

Maxime Gaillard, who in 1891 had bought the parlor of an Italian ice cream merchant to call it stupidly *Maxime,* had the good sense to resell it to two industrious young men. The cook chaveau and the maitre d'hôtel Cornuche hastened to anglicise its name. The anglomania of Parisians in the "Belle Epoque" was as violent as the one driving Gallic teeny-boppers to the land of the Beatles.

For 20 years, *Maxim's* must have been what *Régine, Castel* and *l'Elysée-Matignon* are today—and even more. The great courtesans who could manage their careers better than Christine Keelers of the atomic age, used to borrow a few dozen Louis from Gérard Armeau, king of hunters and hunter of kings, and reimburse him after a wild supper with Léopold II the Prince de Galles, Prince Napoléon or the Grand Duke Serge (who was never forgiven by the Russian nihilists for bestowing a pearl necklace worth a million in gold upon the splendid Augustine de Lierre).

The goddesses of the now faded demi-monde were very comfortable at *Maxim's,* where they reigned over reigning princes. Liane de Pougy—the No. 1 rival of la Belle Otero (who recently died in Nice in poverty)—had inaugurated at *Maxim's* the second revolving door in Paris, (the first was the door of *Café de la Paix*) and created a scandal doing it. Her senses unaccustomed to this gyratory exercise, she left part of her train under a door drum. Paul, the porter responsible for this crime of "lèse-courtisane," was requested to turn in his lobster-red uniform.

Emilienne d'Alençon, Liane Lancy, Renée de Presle, Maud d'Amuseau, Aimienne de Mirecourt, Clémentine de Pibrac and the beautiful equestrian Rita del Rio lacked less intelligence than virtue, while their escorts were quicker with a Louis than repartee and had a taste for hilarious stories.

M. Vaudable, who manages this venerable Parisian institution is seeking a formula that will attract to his red benches a clientele as lively at the end of a "Générale" as during daylight hours. Roger, successor to the famous Albert, may have given the place a new aura in adopting a Mao formal on New Year's Eve 1968, but *Maxim's* remains a grand restaurant, where dignified late dinners, rather than mad suppers, are the norm. Today's chic party girls prefer to take their dates to fashionable bistros located much closer to go-go dance spots. Nevertheless, *Maxim's* still shines bright after a soirée on the right bank, a gala performance at the Opera or even a Sammy Davis Première at the Olympia. Tout-Paris still makes reservations at ANJ. 27-94.

Princess Grace of Monaco, the Maharani of Baroda, Curt Jurgens, Elsa Martinelli, the Rothchilds and Alain Delon may meet there Régine, the high priestess of the contemporary night. She likes to have her supper in style and doesn't hide her weakness for *Maxim's* (she never did comment on the orchestra).

Friday is formal night by order of the management. But on Tuesdays you may flirt with purple and gold, while avoiding the common staircase leading to the less chic room. Your companion may decide with exquisite simplicity that it looks good to have grilled meat at *Maxim's;* in this case we recommend "selle de veau, ou d'agneau" (saddle of veal or mutton) over the too well-known "sole Albert." Remember the sherbert before you part with some 200 francs (for two) in this temple of light memories, always a high spot gastronomique.

la Brasserie Lorraine. place des Ternes, 227-80-04.
Open till 2 a.m. You can choose between the "brasserie" (beer hall) and the more expensive restaurant. You will be served correctly and rapidly in a conventional and calm setting. In the summer you can have your supper on the terrace.

The place isn't original, but you can discuss there the film you just saw on the Champs and not be disturbed by the conversation at the next table. Estimate a minimum of 30 francs a head at the restaurant.

Le Dahu. 10, rue La Trémoille, 359-72-68.
Regularly receives people from the music world. Real or would-be idols, impresarios and art directors dine there after Premières on "crèpes á la provençale" (flap mushrooms) and "brochettes" (broiled meat). The cuisine is good, and the ground level hall is noisy when full. You must manage your con-

versation skillfully so as not to confuse it with the one conducted at the next table. Roughly 35 francs.

Dessirier. 9, place Pereire, 425-74-14.
Service till 1 o'clock is a feat in this quartier Pereire-Champerret, where chefs unanimously turn their aprons in around 10 p.m. Good service and very tasty food is even more unusual. Good for sea food; and don't hesitate to order the dijonnaise rabbit.

L'Elysée-Club. corner of avenues Matignon and Gabriel, BAL. 73-13.
Pierre-Louis now entertains at this restaurant where "Tout-Minuit" (night jet-set) parades. Movie and theatre people, good and neutral cooking (service till 1 a.m.), a check for a least 40 francs per person. It is discreet and calm, and the terrace is very pleasant in the summer.

Le Luigi's. 6, rue lu Colisée, 359-83-46.
Serves till 12:30 only, but gives you the opportunity to sup calmly for about 35 francs—after a movie at an exclusive showcase theatre. The minestrone has been baptised "Italian Minestrone," for all to see the connection of this restaurant with the region beyond the Alps, though it is decorated in British-bar style and managed by a Savoyard (from Savoie). Which doesn't prevent them from featuring on their very fine menu "Cotriade-comme-en-Bretagne" (a fishchowder). (Closed on Sunday)

Rech. 62, av. des Ternes, 380-38-87.
Doesn't have the characteristics of a restaurant for hardened night prowlers. The habitués from *Régine* might be bored here at 1 in the morning. But they can find some very tasty sea-food in this place. The fish is fresh, the camembert cheese gigantic, and the check is 40 francs (or more, depending on the shellfish you order). (Closed in the summer)

Le Stella. corner rue Victor Hugo and rue de la Pompe, 727-60-54.
Has the rare quality of staying open till 2 (unusual in this neighborhood), but after 1:30 count on a cold buffet only. Good brasserie-type food and service for 20 to 25 francs. The clientele is typical XVIth "arrondissement" (precinct), namely models and night-owls who wish to dine peacefully before landing in *Club de l'Etoile*. Sometimes, the Renoma brothers, charles Glenn (of Mayfair) and Alain Dham (of Ramdam) have a late after-business apéritif in this place. (Closed in August)

le Cap Horn. 29, rue de Penthièvre, 359-35-54.
Is managed by the singer, Fred Adison. He offers, till 1 o'clock, after-show supper à la lyonnaise. We recommend their good beaujolais in a pitcher, to wash down a solid repast (40 francs). The latter consists of "boudin grillé aux pommes en l'air" (grilled blood-sausages with potatoes) an enormous "quenelle" (meat ball) and "le saucisson chaud" (hot sausage). (Closed on Sunday)

le Grand Pub. 82, avenue Marceau, 256-20-40.
Serves "panses de brebis farcies" (stuffed sheep's belly) and less original British specialties till 2 a.m. This Parisian pub in a bona fide British setting offers an extensive whiskey list (over 30 brands) and all the beers found on the East and West End. New stronghold of the anglicised night-owl, the *Grand Pub* opened at the end of 1967 behind *le Drugstore* of the Champs-Elysées.

le Grill Marbeuf. 15, rue Marbeuf, 225-22-58.
Doesn't hide its merchandise: beef quarters are shown in a refrigerated chamber with glass walls. Noisy and crowded during "normal" mealtimes, *le Grill* is quiet after eleven. Neat and clean decor without pretentions, good meat, air conditioning. About 25 francs.

la Mamma. 25, rue Marbeuf, 225-08-40.
Isn't intimate or worldly, but offers thirteen varieties of pizza, good fettucini, scampi milanese (breaded) and a "Barbera fruité" (dessert). In this large hall with exposed beams you can eat Italian style till one thirty in the morning.

It is honest for 25 francs. Luckily, the Italian singers don't perform too long; the bathrooms are painted a depressing blue.

le Palmier de Longchamp. 148, av. Victor-Hugo, 727-80-29.
Receives till 1:30 a.m. the night trade of the XIVth arrondissemment: a place to note in this particularly dark part of the neighborhood, where *le Stella* alone once kept watch. We didn't sample this restaurant which opened beginning 1968 across the street from the *Times Square Drugstore,* but we assure you that you and date can dine late and properly there for 50 francs.

le Pub Renault. 53, Champs-Elysées, 256-18-40.
Belongs to the family of drugstores on l'Etoile and Saint-Germain-des-Prés though you will only find there a gadget shop. You can pamper yourself instead, with a "R 16" or an "Alpine" upon getting up from the table.

Located at the end of the Renault exhibition hall, *le Pub* offers a 1900's decor, to which accessories of antique cars have been added. You can dine rapidly till 2 in the morning for less than 20 francs. The hot meals are called "Hot Plates" on the menu to make Anglo-Saxon visitors feel at home. Other good-neighbor dishes are the hamburger sandwich, the cheeseburger, and the shrimp salad bowl.
If you have a desire for something French, you can satisfy it by ordering the "plat du jour": "boeuf gros sel" (beef and vegetables in pot) or other, for 8 or 9 francs.

le Quick. 114, Champs-Elysées, 225-16-10.
Offers sandwiches, hot-dogs, "croque-monsieurs" (Welsh-rarebit ham sandwich) and néons, till 2 a.m. An escalator will softly carry you to the first floor (2nd floor in America) where you will find honest nourishment for 15 or 20 francs (grill service till 1:30) in a quiet room.

AFTER 2 A.M.

---

la Calavados. 40, avenue Pierre-de-Serbie, 359-27-28.
Americanized by the clients of the nearby *George V* to the point of announcing on the menu "dinners-by-candle-light," but still part of the type of Parisian night that sees stragglers gorge themselves with spaghetti during hours when the normal Frenchman washes down with brandy the terrible coffee served at the counter.
The restaurant on the first floor is open till 4 o'clock (estimate 40 to 45 francs). Unrepentant night-owls are mainly familiar with the ground-floor hall where they can eat pretty well—not that it matters—for some 25 francs. The clientele consists of Parisians who are never tired, yet sleep till noon, and wealthy strangers accompanied by ladies in mink coats too light to be real. The usual trio, always there, doesn't bother the American clientele which is used to the assaults of tender guitars. We enjoyed the piano player with the heavy eyelids who unwinds strange lazy dreams on the keyboard. Joe Turner pretends to be asleep, or he may well be asleep, but he plays great.

If you don't feel like a hamburger or two fried eggs ("oeufs au plat"), you can just have a drink. *La Calavados* is your last stop before retiring to sleep or to the sleepy loves of dawn.

La Caravelle. 4, rue Arsène-Houssaye, 359-47-36.
Receives Pathé-Marconi people at lunch and all show-business

at night (open till 6 a.m.). The cooking is the same as at *la Villa d'Este*—almost average. You may eat properly for 20 to 30 francs, unless you stick with the plat du jour. The lounge-chairs are comfortable, the atmosphere quiet enough for the impresarios talking in whispers with young singers or even Jacques Brel. Once in a while, an author-composer will play a few original chords on his guitar. It is rather pleasant and stays calm. If you wish, you can stop for a drink at the bar.

Les Innocents. 6, rue Robert-Estienne (rue Marbeuf), 359-40-70.

Is located on a dead-end street, forgotten ever since the heroic days of the first *Whiskey à Go-go*. Stéphane, who did his apprenticeship at *la Vie Parisienne,* now receives host-clients by a quietly crackling fire. If you don't put money on the table, you may play gin-rummy there just like at home. You can also daydream over a drink or dine peacefully for less than 60 francs for two.

This little restaurant-club; charming, correct and peaceful, is open till 6 a.m. The waiters ask the customers to hold on to their silverware but in their usual friendly way. Especially recommended to those who dream of an evening with friends (strictly Parisian) like in the mountains. . . .

Le 5e avenue. 4, avenue Victor-Hugo, 727-69-46.
Has replaced Potel et Chabot in quarters redecorated by Georges Peynet (a specialist in movie-theatre decoration) in the Colonial American style. Launched at the time this guide was being reprinted, *le 5e avenue* should be staying open till 3 a.m. The fortunate clients of le *Club de l'Etoile* (in the cellar) will have the opportunity to have supper there for about 30 francs.

Le Jour et Nuit. 2, rue de Berry, 359-12-63.
Is air-conditioned, impersonal and refined, but no longer deserves its name. After years of staying open till dawn, it now closes as soon as the sensible after-movie suppers are over.

Le Little Bar. at the corner of rue de Ponthieu and rue du Colisée, 359-94-88.
Stays open all night. You can have breakfast there before going home or munch on a bowl of spaghetti or a couple of hamburgers (15 to 20 francs for a late snack).

A calm and clean room in the basement, a mixed but anonymous clientele on the ground floor. (Closed on Sunday)

Le Petit Berri. 19, rue de Berri, 359-46-10 and 42-46.
Is open 24 hours a day. A clean and plain bistrot: simple meals

served all night. There you can see the girls from the *Lido*, discotheque barmen and taxi drivers. You can fare well for less than 20 francs.

Another **Petit Berry.** (do not confuse them) 37, rue Marbeuf. Is admittedly an anonymous and clean café, open late. You are limited to sandwiches and a cold buffet.

le Snack des arcades du Lido. 78, Champs-Elysées, 225-38-85. (at the entrance of the hall leading to the Lido)
Doesn't look like a restaurant, yet super-nocturnes, night workers and of course *le Lido's* personnel are familiar with its hamburgers, its sandwiches and its omelets. You sit at a counter, but you will be served till 4 a.m.

Clichy/Pigalle/Montmartre

BEFORE 2 A.M.

L'Assommoir. 12, rye Gidardon, 076-55-01.
Is a very charming, semi-luxurious bistrot that has the good sense to spare its clientele trite candlelight dinners: "poulet au citron" (spring chicken with lemon), checkerboard tablecloths and handsome African sculptures adorn the place. You can arrive at this Assommoir till 1:30, it borrowed from Zola only its name, otherwise it is an unpretentious place with tasty specialties: good "pâté de grives" (thrush pie), healthy steaks, fine desserts. For 60 francs you can have dinner for two seated among comedians, musicians and singers. The latter come from the nearby *Moulin de la Galette,* now adapted for television, where they tape Raisner's "Têtes de bois" and a few Sacha-Shows.

We would like to make a note that this restaurant is located on the more "villagy" side of Montmartre, but has nothing in common with the Butte where tourists and broad jokes thrive. (Closed on Monday)

L'Auberge du XVIIIe. 6, rue Caulaincourt, 387-64-78.
Will stay open only long enough for you to cross the street immediately after the show at the Gaumont Palace. This is a restaurant where one comes in for a very late dinner rather than supper.

As midnight nears, your chances to be served the tasty "bourride de la maison" (fish-stew Provençale) grow poorer. But you can drown your sorrows in the "soupe de poisson" (fish chowder), the "moule farcies" (stuffed mussels), the "escargots au Chablis" (snails in wine) and the "poularde feuilletée" (fowl in fluffy paste). A friendly greeting, peacefulness and good wines. It will cost you at least 40 francs, but you won't regret it.

Les Cadets de Gascogne. 4, place du Tertre, 606-71-73.
Has a grand and lively star, Dédé! This robust songstress is without a doubt thoroughly familiar with the repertory of Montmartre-songs—even the worst—but she also knows how to make sea lovers dream. She knows more sea songs than an old trawler. True that she was singing for years at Saint-Malo. . . .

Dinner or supper at *les Cadets de Gascogne* costs 30 or 40 francs . . . unless you flirt with the great vintage wines which the owner collects passionately. (Open every day; Closed during January and February.)

Charlot Ier 138 bis, boulevard de Clichy, 522-47-08.
Is rarely included with the itinerary of gastronomers-who-are-not-sleepy, though the fish and shellfish are very fresh, and service—till 2 a.m.—as swift as it is courteous. Estimate 40 francs minimum, it's fair enough.

Le Coup le Frein. 88, rue Lepic, 076-90-06.
Is worth a stop on your way up la Butte. Further up you will have trouble finding a discreet restaurant where you can chat intimately with your companion.

The place is kept by charming young people. Service is nice and slow, the decor romantic and baroque. You can sup there till two in the morning, sometimes later, with background music ground out by a player-piano.

Healthy and sometimes diverting bistrot-de-luxe cooking at moderate prices. You may exceed the moderate fixed-meal price, but you won't pay more than 25 or 30 francs. (Closed on Tuesday)

Chez Haynes. 3, rue Clauzel, 878-40-63.
The cuisine is "meridional" . . . for New Yorkers. The Southern chef, who leaves his oven around 1 o'clock, cooks "travers de porc" (pork chops), chili and Fried chicken with a Louisiana or Mexican accent. Jazz musicians and spicy-sauce lovers come regularly to this good American restaurant in Paris. Roughly 20 to 30 francs. (Closed on Sunday)

La Mangeoire. 17, rue Ganneron, 387-10-95.
Its clientele is mixed only to the extent that a few young women (often virile looking) arrive in the company of gentlemen (too sweet to be interested in the weaker sex). The young men who swoon in masculine company choose the darkness of the lower level, but you can have a quiet and pleasant after-theatre supper on the ground floor. Fixed-price meals for 15 francs estimate 20 to 25 F. à la carte.

la Rose des Pierrots de la Butte. 41, rue Ganneron, 387-10-95.
Stays open late and doesn't offer anything costly . . . nor good (we had there tripe that obviously came straight from a can.) Formerly we had found this place appealing, but when we returned just before writing this note, it was merely noisy. We concede that at the time a party of ten people, among whom were two vociferous ladies, had monopolised a row of tables. About 20 francs.

le Wagon Montmartrois. 17, avenue Rachel, 387-66-12.
Is "Chez Louis." It is nearly impossible to have dinner or supper in this little unadorned restaurant—open till at least one—without noticing this coleric and friendly man, constantly on the move and ceaselessly berating his wife, who is for all that an excellent cook. One special night, treat yourself to "langoustine grillée" (grilled lobster). For 40 or 45 francs you may prefer the tasty "plat-maison" (specialty of the house). On escapades with a woman other than your wife, this place offers the reassuring advantage of parking on a dead-end street where nobody will recognize your car.

le Wepler. 14, place Clichy, 522-53-24.
Has had its moment of glory, and is now a large "brasserie" (beer hall) with efficient service. Neutral and honest cooking till about 12:30. Estimate 25 to 30 francs. If you just want a drink, *le Wepler* is open to 2 a.m.

AFTER 2 A.M.

Le Bistrot du Roy. 4, villa St-Michel (corner av. de St-Ouen), 627-67-51.
Feeds till dawn comedians and habitués of the nearby *Bar Belge*, who get hungry drinking beer. The chef forgets over his stoves the frantic yé-yés that introduced him to the night. James Thibault (one of the two James of the Palladium) serves

fine food in a XVIth century setting. A small grilled rooster (coquelet grillé) preceded by "tarte à l'onion" (onion pie) and followed by a "tarte chaude" (hot pie) will cost you some 30 or 35 francs, including wine and service. (Closed on Sunday)

La Cloche d'Or. 3, rue Mansart, 874-48-88.
Really serves till 6 in the morning. If you are famished at dawn, you have a choice between "petite salé" (pickled porc), "jambon en croûte" (ham sandwich) and "boeuf mode" (pork & beef marinated in brandy, then braised in wine) on the main menu if you are not satisfied with just a "gratinée" (prepared au gratin) or a "croque-monsieur" (sandwich variation). Specializing in a clientele from the song and comedy world, it is nevertheless as well known by night folks as *Lipp*, It owes its success to the efforts and tenacity of Henri Marc, a native of Auvergne, who in 1928 took over this concern where he had previously served as head waiter. He passed it on to his son Robert, who knows "Tout-Paris" yet still shops at les Halles.

Before the war, Kessel, Marcel Achard, and Trenet had first started frequenting *la Cloche* and they can still be seen there today. Piaf was often observed there and now you can meet Richard Anthony, Hallyday, Antoine, Claude François and numerous comedians. In order not to be disturbed, they move to the back of the room on the raised part of the restaurant and discuss their future acts with musicians and journalists.

Estimate 30 to 45 francs for a proper supper in this restaurant set in a rustic "normand" atmosphere. This is reasonable for simple food of good quality, so much more appreciated when enhanced by their quiet and courteous service.

La Dinanderie. 7, rue de Cheroy, 387-23-15.
Receives actors of le théâtre Hébertot with candlelight. Located in a quarter that is rather dead after midnight, this restaurant has the good taste to stay open till at least three o'clock.

An intimate and vaguely normand décor, onion pie and "crêpe de langoustine" (lobster filled crepe), kind reception and pleasant service—all for about 40 francs—which still seems somewhat expensive to us, but this doesn't prevent Marina Vlady, Odile Versois, Delphine Seyrig, Alain Delon and Jean Rochefort from coming by regularly.

If you feel like having a drink in a quiet little discotheque, you can go down to the mini-club located under the restaurant.

La Fringale. 60, rue Notre-Dame-de-Lorette, 874-96-79.
Doesn't suffer from its proximity to Pigalle. The decor is

without pretentions but the place is clean and the service friendly.

In a neighborhood of restaurants that resort to payoffs, the little *Fringale* offers till dawn a meal for 16 francs. It is totally devoid of gastronomic illusions, but it has good food and fair prices. A peaceful an picturesque clientele: "boys" and "girls" from the *Folies-Bergères* or the *Casino de Paris*, dancers and strip-teasers who come in to have a plate of spaghetti after the cabarets close. They don't even take the time to remove their false eyelashes and stage make-up. (Closed on Wednesday)

Michou (chez Mme Untel). 80, rue des Maryrs, 606-16-04.

Has changed its decor to a rip-roaring 1920's: red and black, mirrors and looking-glasses. Once again open all night, this very charming restaurant gives you a chance to dine for some 35 francs (which is really moderate, but you can come with a model or a cover-girl. Michou welcomes the ladies with a courtesy often forgotten by sanely hetero-sexual restaurant-keepers. Very Parisian.

La Pizza. 10, boulevard de Clichy, 606-03-35.

You won't easily find something better. The head-waiter is charming. The cuisine appropriate. The prices possible (estimate 15 francs). The clientele quiet. (Service till 4 a.m.)

Proust. 68, rue des Martyrs, 878-43-31.

Remembers the lost "cassoulet" (pork and beans) and rediscovers the forgotten "truffe" (truffel).

M. Lamazère, a Toulousain (and ex-prestidigitator) manages this "day and night" restaurant, oddly set in a hôtel. His "foie gras" (goose liver) is well-known among nocturnes who still appreciate good food, and his truffles are wonderfully scented. With the exception of the classic *Cloche d'Or,* this is the only unequivocally insomniac restaurant in Pigalle that we can recommend without qualms.

Palais-Royal/Le Marais

BEFORE 2 A.M.

L'Ambassade d'Auvergne. 22, rue du Grenier-Saint-Lazare, 272-31-22.

Is owned by an Italian who switched from spaghetti to "potée" (stewed pork and lard) and "tripoux" (a mutton-tripes concoction) ever since his marriage to a girl from Auvergne. The "plates-maison" are as solid as the beams running through the ceiling. You can dine for less than 30 francs in this ambassade where they serve you beautiful "truites aux lardons" (trout and bacon) and a tasty "poitrine de veau farcie" (stuffed breast of veal).

Le Bistroquet. 26, quai du Louvre, 236-49-52.
Unfortunately serves only to 11 p.m. on quiet evenings. This charming rather expensive restaurant (be prepared for 100 francs for two) was once very fashionable, but no longer attracts evening society. For those leaving the movies rather early with a yearning for a palatable pastry.

Le Brignolet. 29, rue de Montpensier, 742-71-42.
Offers steaks grilled on a log fire for 12 francs, and an after-show meal for 25 francs. A few show-biz habitués, a fireplace in the back of the room, and quiet.

Le Grill de la Plantation. 50, rue de Richelieu, 742-48-11.
On your way out of the Comédie-Française you can have supper for less than 30 francs. The grilled steaks are good and coffee is on the house. Instead of leaving conventionally through rue Richelieu, take the hidden staircase that leads down to the "club" where you might meet some very pretty girls.

Le Quetsch. 6, rue des Capucines, 073-06-91.
Offers a light supper for 20 or 25 francs on your way out of le Théâtre des Capucines or le Daunou. Located in a business district that sleeps deeply after midnight, this restaurant, neat and unpretentious, serves until 1:30. (Closed on Sunday)

La Sellerie. 8, rue Boudreau, 073-40-19.
Receives many comedians until at least 2 in the morning and often much later. Jean Poiret, the actor Jean Valmence, and Gérard Sabbath (of les Compagnons de la Chanson) are three of the 7 shareholders who opened this hippy-style restaurant, only two minutes from l'Olympia and le Théâtre Edouard II. Marcel Achard, Jacques Martin, Jean Yvanne and Jacques Brel often meet there after the show for "oeufs pochés au vin" (poached eggs in wine) and "carré d'agneau" (loin of lamb).

The place is quiet and relaxing the cooking is as honest as the prices: 25 to 30 francs. (Closed on Sunday and in August)

Le Tokay. 43, rue de Montpensier, 742-32-32.
Is managed by a very Parisian Roumanian gypsy, Lydia Goulesco. Good Hungarian and Russian cuisine, violins and cymbalum, a Central European and Danubian mood will easily make you forget the amount on the check (40 to 50 francs). Better make a reservation, though; you will be served promptly after a show. (Closed on Sunday and from the end of July to the end of August.)

AFTER 2 A.M.

Viva Maria. 8, rue de Beaujolais, 236-38-59.
A charming little restaurant with candlelight, opened after the release of the film of the same name starring B.B. and Jeanne Moreau. The cuisine is of course Spanish-Mexican. The Mexican salad is fresh and spicy, the paëlla de Murcie (how does it differ from the Valencian one?) is plentiful, well garnished and can serve as a main dish.

The cook, who stays by his stoves till dawn, has a nice Iberian voice, which he shares with the clients. Some of his dishes are a little too pungant, but not his voice. Estimate about 35 francs. Open to 5 or 6 a.m. (Closed Tuesday)

La Pizza. 37, rue de Montpensier, 742-82-80.
Is open till dawn and is reasonably priced. Men can safely venture in this little night-restaurant with no risk to their dignity, but the regular female customers have a tendency to spend their nights among women.

Les Halles

The transfer of les Halles to Rungis puts the neighborhood's restaurant situation in a new light: some of them seem to want to hold out, but we cannot predict the look this IIe arrondissement will have in 1970.

L'Alsace aux Halles. 16, rue Coquillière, 236-74-24.
Is the least noisy of the restaurants located along rue Coquil-

lière. The workers at les Halles don't venture much there. They probably don't approve of the pretentious unsightliness of the decor, consisting of varnished barrels and wrought iron. It has its advantages, since you can come in with a lady wearing a very open and very "mini" dress without having to endure the gibes of habitués.

There is no risk of grand culinary adventures at *l'Alsace aux Halles:* the cauliflower is neither better nor worse than at *Lipp's.* Roughly 30 F.

L'Epi d'Or 25, rue Jean-Jacques Rousseau, 236-38-12.

Is open from 11 p.m. to 3 in the afternoon, which means you can have "jambon de pays" (ham) or an "omelette" after all other restaurants have quit for the night. Nobody bothers with elegance in this bistrot where the workers from les Halles mix with "clochards," students on the spree and night-owls with pangs.

The lighting brings out the worst in make-up. Do come only with friends who won't care about the décor and who want to eat at modest prices (most dishes are under 7 francs).

Chez Guyomard. 5, rue du Jour, 236-94-81.

The decor is sadly impersonal. It is not necessary to come with a Marie-Chantal: robust butchers come in for drinks at the bar after having spent the day carrying quarters of beef which leave bloody marks on their white shirts.

Many merchants from les Halles patronize this all-night *Guyomard.* You can have supper either on the ground floor or on the first, and if you wish, you may simply have a "fondue bourguignonne." Very fresh shells and fish, a bouillabaise (fish-soup of Marseille) any Marseillais would be proud of, a good Sancerre de Chavignol, rosé and refreshing. The place closes on Saturday and Sunday during the summer, but in the winter it is open every day. From 20 to 35 francs, depending on your appetite.

Le Pied de Cochon. 6, rue Coquillière, 236-11-75.

Offers till dawn platters of "cochonailles" (dressed pork), exquisite meat and seafood to sometimes "dressy" clients, which doesn't prevent the strongmen at the counter from eyeing the mini-skirted filles.

The menu is long and so is the service-time. The clients, who are occasionally noisy and vulgar, create a disagreable banquet-atmosphere. This place is often appreciated by out-of-towners who love to laugh, a napkin around their neck (it costs them about 30 francs), but all depends on the oysters (beautiful and fresh).

Robert Vattier. 14, rue Coquillière, 236-51-60 and 53-93.
Proudly declares "food comes first, decorations second," as if they couldn't coexist. The decor isn't too sordid (as far as les Halles go), the room on the first floor is as clean as it is drab.

The "gratinées," the seafood, the stuffed mussels ("moules farcies") and the meats are quite decent. The french-fries are sometimes less so and taste slightly greasy-spoon. The atmosphere is definitely less vulgar than at the nearby *Pied de Cochon*. The "addition" (check) varies from 25 to 35 francs. Checks are not accepted. (Closed in August)

Ile Saint-Louis/Ile de la Cite

Les Anysetiers du Roy. 61, rue Saint-Louis en l'Isle, 033-02-70.
Smell of the grass in Provence late at night. You can drop in without notice until one in the morning and then you can make a reservation till dawn.

Located in a beautiful house in the XVIIe (arrondissement), *les Anysetiers* offers a meal for 40 francs, wine and service included. The owner is courteous and discreet. (Closed on Monday)

La Colombe. 4, rue de la Colombe, 633-37-08.
Has inspired Brigitte Bardot with a beautiful compliment: "One forgets Paris at *la Colombe*, but when in Paris, one doesn't forget *la Colombe*."

The restaurant is located in a XIIIth century house, expanded in the XVth. Michel and Belein Valette discontinued their floor-shows in 1964, but the singers who had their start there still come in regularly. They are Jean Ferrat, Guy Beart, Pierre Perret . . . Michel Valette handles the clients personally till 2 a.m. while his wife supervises the kitchen. Robert J. Courtine, the man who revised the monumental *Larousse Gastronomique*, takes issue with the name borrowed from Sarah Bernhardt . . . but there is nothing else to reproach *la Colombe's* beautiful menu. (Estimate 40 francs if you don't follow the fixed-price dinners at 30 and 35 francs.)

To your elegant and refined companion you may suggest "truite fumée" (smoked trout), "caneton aux pêches" (duckling with peaches) and "tarte tatin" (caramelized apple tart). You may take a table in one of the pleasant ground floor or first floor rooms, but when the night is mild we recommend a reservation on the terrace—not very spacious but one of the most attractive in Paris. (Closed on Sunday)

Le Franc-Pinot. 1, quai Bourbon, 033-46-98.
Offers to strangers who come down its stairs a superb cave dug out in 1661, a variety-show, suavely filtered lighting. It will cost you at least 150 francs for a tete-à-tête supper—service till 2—but there is a dance floor where you can twirl after the show ends (at about 1 a.m.).

L'Orangerie. 28, rue St-Louis-en-l'Isle, 633-93-98.
Has enough clients to stay open till 3 a.m. and never take an evening off. Owned and financed by Jean-Claude Brialy, this tastefully decorated restaurant is managed by Gérard Ferry, who started the charming *Maschou* on the buttress of the Tour de Suquet in Cannes. Many comedians, a snobbish and sophisticated clientele appreciate the liberally served fresh fruit and vegetable hors-d'oeuves ("crudités") and the beautiful grilled steaks. This charming and distinguished place offers de luxe fixed-price meals: starting at 50 francs, wine and service included.

Le Chapitre. 36, rue St.-Louis-en-Isle, 633-56-09.
Quouiquette Terrail (we are not aware of any other given name), sister of Claude Terrail, of *la Tour d'Argent,* recently established herself in the beautiful vaulted caves of la Tassée. Candlelight, grilled steaks and exotic dishes accompanied by mysterious sauces. Comedians such as Claude Rich and Delphine Seyrig, and customers as discreet as the lighting. Estimate 90 or 100 francs for two. (Closed on Sunday)

Saint-Germain-des-Pres Montparnasse/Champ de Mars

BEFORE 2 A.M

Lipp. 151, boulevard Saint-Germain, 548-53-91.
Rates not only because of its herrings from the Baltic, its sauerkraut and its "boeuf mode" (marinated beef and pork, boiled in white wine). Roger Cazes, successor to his father, who created the place, isn't infatuated with gastronomic in-

tricacies. With courtesy and firmness he manages a most Parisian brasserie—an annex to the Palais Bourbon, publishing houses and theatres. The brasserie *Lipp* owes its name to the brave Alsacien who preferred to work hard in a small room on boulevard Saint-Germain, rather than stay in his own country under German rule (after 1870). M. Lippman didn't suspect that in 1920 a man from Auvergne would buy the place (5 years of credit payments) and send it off fast enough for Léon-Paul Fargue to devote a chapter to it in *Piéton de Paris*.

Marcellin Cazes, born in Lauguiole (Aveyron) to a very poor family with eight children, was hired out to farmers at eleven. He started his own conquest of Paris by delivering coal. He later was a water-heaver for an entrepreneur of "baths at home" and a waiter, until his savings covered the price of a meager café on boulevard Voltaire. After a laborious ascension he established himself in Saint-Germain-des-Prés and six years later he had expanded from ten to one hundred tables by annexing the penthouse, the backyard and the porter's apartment. Léon-Paul Fargue, who would infallibly arrive about midnight for a glass of mineral water, was the leading figure of the place. but you could also meet there Antoine de Saint-Exupéry, André Maginot (of the line) André Tardieu and Léon Jouhaux. Edouard Herriot was so mad about the Baltic-herrings that he usually took some home! Actors started coming in, in the days of le Vieux Colombier, after Jacques Copeau and Louis Jouvet.

The politicians remained faithful to *Lipp*. Roger Cazes, who took over after the death of his father, receives Georges Pompidou as well as François Mitterand, the government as well as the anti-government. Late into the night—until he can relax and take a bite himself—Roger seats his clients with expertness, alternating ministers, stars, journalists, writers and anonymous customers.

Lipp serves till 1 a.m. It is not a club, and anybody can come in, but we suggest you arm yourself with patience. You may have to wait three quarters of an hour to be seated, but you may give up as soon as you get there because a sign at the entrance usually warns you of the waiting time.

The clientele at *Lipp* has grown younger over the years, mainly because children of illustrious clients frequent the place as well (usually leaving the check for papa). Roger Cazes sometimes knows three or four generations of a family and receives young people to whom he used to serve grenadine syrup.

All this shouldn't make you forget that you are eating at *Lipp*. The menu doesn't offer a wide selection but the food is remarkably steady: the house ignores les Halles and calls upon loyal suppliers. The same pastry shop has been delivering pâtisserie since the creation of *Lipp,* while the present butcher and the greengrocer have been with *Lipp* for 25 years. If you are Marlène Dietrich, Alain Delon, Darryl Zanuck, Eddie Barclay, Eddie Mitchell (or any anonymous "Lippien"), you probably won't come to Lipp for a complete and perfectly organized meal. We recommend their beer, their "vins-maison," their herring, beef-mode, roast pork, munster and pies; and we remind you that service is neither included nor mentioned on the check (which will be at least 30 francs). At *Lipp,* the tip is considered a reward, and the client alone can determine the amount. (Closed on Monday, and during July)

Le Bistrot de Paris. 33, rue de Lille, 548-32-44.
Was opened in a 1900 décor (signed Slavik) by Michel Olivier, who is the cook at *le Grand Véfour,* on television. *Le Bistrot de Paris* would have had no place in this guide had Michel Olivier not decided, at the end of 1967, to serve till 11 p.m. As a result, you can arrive there after the first show at the movies, sit at a table till 1 in the morning and have an excellent dinner in this "bistrot de luxe" (about 100 francs for two).

The warm welcome given by Michel Olivier, the high quality of the "Filet à la diable" (seasoned, breaded and grilled fowl, with sauce à la diable) the "pot au feu en vessie" (French stock pot), the "poulet au fromage" (chicken with cheese) and the wines largely justify the check. Especially if you enjoy the proximity of Grace and Rainier of Monaco, Marcel Achard, Elizabeth Taylor, Peter O'Toole, Catherine Deneuve or Pierre Perret . . . (Closed on Sunday)

La Closerie des Lilas. corner boulevard Montparnasse and avenue de l'Observatoire, 326-70-50.
The style is classical, comfortable and impersonal, but the service reminds you at times of an overfull brasserie (beer hall) rather than a large restaurant. A piano player entertains at supper without interrupting businessmen and well-to-do out-of-towners who come in with their family or friends.

A nice menu. Though you could be rightfully disappointed by the "mullet à l'oseille" (mullet with sorel) and the "rosé-maison"—actually one of the least expensive wines. The standard courses are good and the prices relatively light.

La Coupole. 102, boulevard de Montparnasse, 326-95-90.
Offers till 3:30 a large brasserie-menu and good lamb curries. It is an immense *"Lipp* de Montparnasse" (but more impersonal) that opened in a coal depot at the close of the mad years. You may feel lost during the noisy dinner hours, but the place doesn't lack charm at supper time. If you look up, you will discover frescos by Othon Friesz, or you can watch the com-

ings and goings of the new generation of Montparnos, the sculptor César for one. A half-bohemian and half-elegant clientele intermixed with foreigners. You can have supper for 20 francs if you follow the chef's suggestions, but be prepared to pay 30 francs, just in case you don't.

Le Fiacre. 4, rue du Cherche-Midi, 548-09-79.
Closes at two in the morning. The police figure that young men who spend their time in the company of other men need their sleep, though Louis, who bought the place in 1950 on Boris Vlan's advice, keeps his house well. Well enough for the first floor to be a restaurant where Tout-Paris meets, where you can find (normal) men and (normal) women who usually dine at Lipp's or in any other perfectly "moral" place. The masculine mass at the ground-floor bar may frighten hardened heteros, but they won't lose their virile virtue by brushing past these "minets" who are interested in their kind only. Women are mystified by it but don't take offense. They are delighted to find Cardin and Laroche on the first floor, with a few ravishing models.

Louis, who started at *Maxim's* and worked at *Fouquet's,* now rules over 12 tables only; better make a reservation after 9 p.m. He bought a nearby cleaning store but couldn't acquire the intermediary buildings that would have enabled him to create a Super-Fiacre.

Gastronomes don't meet a Louis' but you can dine quite correctly for some 35 or 40 francs, in his soberly redecorated restaurant. You may come with a very sophisticated lady or with a "minette" (hip girl, see "minet" in this book's dictionary) from *chez Castel.* They jerk furiously on the small dance-floor surrounded by tables.

Le Baobab. 7, rue de l'Université, 548-08-80.
All the specialties of Afrique Noise at very Parisian prices— about 45 F. per person. Service till 1 a.m.

Le Bastringue Jaune. 42, rue Jacob, 222-36-75.
Is more remarkable for the fact that you won't become jaundiced by the check. The walls are a jaundiced-yellow and so are the oilclothes the waiters' uniforms and even the french-fries and the white wine. The young and enterprising George Huet has decided to feed his very Parisian contemporaries "soles meunières" (pan fried sole) or "soles frites" (deep fried), preceded by "bigorneaux" (periwinkles) and followed by delectable pastries. Driven out of *le Point Rouge* by flames that totally charred the place, and a specialist in avant-garde furni-

ture-on-sale, he has already seen among his customers Marc Bohan and Tout-Saint-Germain (the quartier's jet set) reflected in his antique mirrors.

La Belle Polonaise. 21, rue de la Gâîté, 326-68-50.
Has made a pleasant change in its decor. Meet there before a great event at Bobino, buy cigarettes and even dine there . . . if you aren't invited to dine with the star of the show or with his co-performers "à l'Américanine" (short acts preceding the star performance) to *les Iles Marquises.* For two, the check won't exceed 45 francs.

La Bricole. 5, rue Perronet, 222-87-53.
Is a pleasant restaurant with no culinary illusions. It stays open till 2 and is only moderately expensive. A meal goes for 50 to 60 francs for two.

La Brocherie. 3, rue Saint-Benoît, 222-49-92.
Gives relatively-broke Germano-pratins a chance to dine late and linger on for 25 francs. It is less luxurious and less expensive than the *Bistingo,* less Parisian than *le Bioboquet.* In the summer, a long row of tables on the sidewalk, where it is difficult to find a place on a mild day. (Closed on Monday)

L'Epicerie. 1, rue Saint-Benoît, 548-01-06.
Has student prices. You can dine there till 1:30 for less than 5 francs. (Closed on Tuesday)

Les Iles Marquises. 15, rue de la Gaîté, 326-66-47.
Are packed after the Premières at the *Bobino,* but generally serve till 1 o'clock only. For 40 francs you can have a "maritime" supper to follow your rediscovery of Ferrat, Ferré or Brassens. Beautiful oysters, fresh fish and waiters in sailor oufits. (Closed on Sunday)

La Malène. 26, rue St-Benoît, 548-62-43.
Was the meeting of the "Paroissiens" during the great era of Saint-Germian-des-Prés, when the jazz at *Club Saint-Germain* didn't anticipate the jerks danced at the *Bilboquet.*

They serve until 1:30 pizza and Italian dishes, washed down with Corsican wines (Patrimonio is 12 francs). A few terrace-tables to be taken by storm in the summer; a bar where the neighborhood old-timers still meet. A clientele of foreign intellectuals, fairly rich students and young ladies wearing miniskirts (notwithstanding their extensive reading). Estimate 20 francs.

La Mamma. 6, rue Montfaucon, 326-08-24.
Receives Italian-style till 1:30. Same program as at *la Mamma* of rue Marbeuf. Estimate 20 to 25 F.

Le Petit Zinc. 25, rue Buci, 033-79-34.
Is open till three in the morning. You may meet there Antoine and other idols, who come after their singing performance to have a quiet supper in the first floor hall. Pleasant bistrot setting despite the somewhat lugubrious lighting; good, simple and steady food. The check is moderate for a place in this category: 20 to 25 francs. While sipping a kir at the bar, you will have time to hesitate, before your guests arrive, between the "poule au pot" (boiled fowl), "boeuf bourguignon" and "le gigot-flageolets" (leg of mutton with red kidney beans) the specialties of the house.

La Pizza Saint-Germain. 22, rue St-Benoît, 548-28-12.
Receives in its two halls, students, tourists and a neighborhood crowd. The mood is not intimate and you rub elbows at the tables, but the clientele is quiet and the prices make you forget the paper tablecloths. The price of a bottle of Beaujolais is half as much as at *le Bilboquet* and you can dine for 15 to 20 F. Pizza, onion steak, "escalope milanaise" "tagliatelle:" none more than 7 francs per serving. The service keeps up its high standard till 1 a.m.

Pop Hot. 12, rue Grégoire-de-Tours, 033-82-87.
Hairy young men grill the meat till one in the morning, for a few foreign co-eds piled up around a big "rustic" table. You will be less crowded on the first floor. They charge for dinner 20 francs.

Le Port-Saint-Germain. 155, boulevard Saint-Germain, 548-22-66.
Is open till 1:30. Situated within a stone's throw from *Lipp*, it is tranquil and comfortable and decorated with "nordic" woodwork. You will meet there neither heads of state nor big stars; just foreigners and well to do students who have the courtesy to speak low.

Where there is a "Port" there must be fish. The "soupe tropézienne," a little too clear, makes you yearn for *l'Auberge des Maures* and *les Mouscardins,* but it is as good as any such soup served in the fashionable bistrots at Saint-Tropez. Delicious "dordades" (seabream) with herbs. Roughly 20 francs per person for a light but honest supper.

Il Theatro. 38, rue de Bui, 033-40-07.

Offers you the opportunity to have a quick supper at the bar, for 20 or 25 francs. It is overly crowded during dinner hours, but rather quiet after 11 p.m.: service till 1:30. Fifteen varieties of pizza, Italian specialties and wines, good coffee.

Vagenende. 142, boulevard Saint-Germain, 326-68-18.

There you can have supper for less than 20 francs in an amazing 1900 setting. More than the quasi-familiar dishes, we recommend the woodwork, the turn-of-the-century Gramophone, and a superb music box which you may be fortunate enough to hear. Closing time changes, but you are served till at least 12:30.

Le Wagon Salon. 8, rue des Ciseaux, 633-69-49.

The owner, Jean Garel, is one of the best meat grillers in Paris. His "crudités à base de fenouil" (raw hors-d'oeuvres with a base of fennel) and "chou-fleur crus" (raw cauliflower) are amusing. For dessert, order his snow-eggs; you will find it nowhere else.

From 8 to 11 p.m. the clientele is neither very interesting nor very young. But after midnight, you might possibly meet Brigitte Bardot, Jean-Pierre Cassel or Belmondo there. It is safer to make a reservation and while you are at it reserve the "petite salle" near the kitchen. It has a capacity of 2.

Dinners: 30 to 35 F. Service till 2 p.m. (Closed on Sunday)

AFTER 2 A.M.

Le Bistingo. 3, rue St.-Benoît, 222-45-30.

Has become the restaurant of the most straggling of night-stragglers, an after hours meeting place for jazz musicians, night professionals and clients of spots that close at daybreak. Long-waves-Hubert, ex-king of broadcasting station "Europe 1," decided to restore this spot, where the food had been weaker than the prices, to its rightful place in the night-world. Right after his marriage to Corinne Piccoli, he set about this task together with Carlos (Sylvie Vartan's secretary), whose jolly chubbiness betrays his immoderate taste for food.

In grand style, Maurice Casanova and Rolland Pazzo di Borgo had endowed *le Bistingo* with an endless bar before handing it over to Huber and Carlos. From 8 p.m. to 8 a.m., you can dine for some 20 to 25 francs, while waiting for the inevitable "boeuf" (special treat) offered by popular, jazz, and rhythm and blues musicians. The business could be a profitable one if Hubert and Carlos are careful to prevent the fauna that killed *la Cage* and *le Stardust* from overrunning their place. For the moment they have a good hold on their young and pleasantly varied clientele, among which Sacha Distel and Eddie Barclay aren't likely to venture with suit-and-tie.

Chez Castel. 15, rue Princesse, 326-90-23.
Jean Castel entertains Johnny Hallyday, Françoise Hardy, Gilbert Bécaud, Richard Anthony (and all-those-whose-names- appear-in-the-paper) in his 1900's—style dining room, where you eat better than you might expect. For 50 to 60 francs you can have a satisfying supper—at least as good (?) as at *Lipp*.

Le-Saint-Hilaire. 24, rue Vavin, 003-90-95.
Had a catastrophic inauguration on New Year's Eve 1967, but was "operational" a month later. François-Patrice, who ten years ago hadn't done well in the "croque-monsieur" (sandwich variety) business on rue de Ponthieu, has had a successful debut in the more serious night restaurant business. He offers his many loyal customers very fine suppers and (during the summer) all the pleasures of an outdoor garden-terrace.

A strange blue luminosity and stained-glass windows, with facets cut by a mad diamond-cutter, give this spacious and intimate restaurant a unique and definite charm. An Urbini brother (of Saint-Tropez and Mégève) is always on the premises, but be careful before you call him by his first name. The restaurant is run by identical twins.

Strictly reserved for steady clientele (the beautiful and inflexible Coraline will accept only the highly recommended and qualified). The restaurant closes at the wee hours of the morning. You can order unembarrassedly a sandwich at 5 a.m. or have breakfast with François-Patrice before returning dutifully home through the first traffic jams of the day. (50 or 60 francs for a "real meal") During those late hours when women grow tender, we suggest you take a break between two frantic dances by the restaurant's fireplace. The winding staircase is steep, but the big red bench is soft enough for whispered negotiations on the conditions of surrender. . . . (Closed on Sunday)

Le King-Club. 17, rue de l'Echaudé, 633-00-24.
Contains two restaurants connected to Albert Minski's red discotheque by an inner staircase. You don't have to be a member of *le King Club* in order to pass through the heavy wrought-iron gate and the curtain of hot air at the entrance. The local Cerberus grants entry to distinguished or properly escorted people who have had the foresight to make a reservation.

Luxurious, baroque and comfortable, the two restaurants of *le King Club* have reconciled gastronomers with post-midnight cooking. Prices—the same on the first and second floors—are not those of "gargottes" (luncheonettes) for famished revellers, yet you can have a remarkably good meal there for 45 to 60 francs. We warmly recommend the "fritots au fromage" (a cheese dish), "sole au plat" (baked sole with butter & wine) "gigot" (leg of mutton), and all the desserts, especially the delicious "mousse au chocolat" spiced with whiskey.

Albert Minski spent a fortune creating his night-life complex in a XVIIth century house that needed new foundations. He decorated the first floor in a medieval mood and included real stained-glass windows and sculpture on wood. He assigned the walls of the second floor to Archiquille, a painter who can make concrete shimmer. He himself took charge of the installation of the giant aquarium. . . . This night-time Captain Nemo has a passion for submarine depths, and for fish streaked with colors like exotic butterflies. In the aquarium, protected by armoured glass (he isn't about to leave seven tons of water to the mercy of a practical joker), he succeeded in creating peaceful coexistence among a variety of strange creatures from the South Seas. The continuous exchange of 7,000 liters of salt water is costly, but not as costly as the tragic results of the aquatic duels that took place at first. Before they learned to live together, *King's* wonderful fish devoured each other cheerfully or fell into fatal depressions. At the price of rare fish, (each 150 to 3,000 francs) these deaths threatened the house with bankruptcy.

Charles Aznavour, Claude François, Johnny Hallyday, Leon Zitrone, Fernand Reynaud and even the vicontesse de Noailles have spent a couple of hours on the third floor. Minski furnished it with two antique billiard tables, and Darry Cowl, ex-champion of ducks-and-drakes on the green table, has made quite a few thrilling breaks there. You may have to wait for a table (6 to 9 F. per drink at the aquarium bar), but while you wait, you can play a game of pool—a welcome change from pin ball.

Hippolyte; le Club des croulants. (the club for squares). corner boulevard Saint-Germain and rue de Seine, 326-96-36.

Kept by Claude, a former employee of the *King Club*. You can have a good supper for two for 80 or 90 francs, and a late snack for even less.

Only their tangos and songs of the 1900's justify the name on the sign. Cute little "minettes" (see "minet") from Saint-Germain-des-Prés readily accept an invitation to quiet their hunger pangs in this quiet and well-kept restaurant, open till 6 a.m. It's also an "in" spot for night workers: disc-jockeys, doormen, barmen, etc.

L'Echaudé. corner rue de l'Echaudé and Bourbon-le-Château, 033-79-02.

Open till 5, later on Saturday. The not-too-broke-beatnicks eat spaghetti there, next to insomniac students who want to spend less than 30 francs for two. The clientele is young and "du quartier" (from the neighborhood), the white wine is pleasantly scented, and old posters decorate walls that have yellowed. (Closed on Sunday)

La Mamma. 46, rue Vavin, 633-17-92.

Open till dawn. In a long room, they serve you honest but standard Italian food . . . same as at *la Mamma* of rue Marbeuf or of rue Montfaucon, since they are all branches of the same firm. About 25 F.

Le O.K. Bar. 27, rue Bréa, 326-64-85.

Looks empty at 11 p.m. but fills up at about 3 or 4 in the morning. The tardy night-owls of Montparnasse have a scanty but good meal there after "normal" revellers go to bed. At the approach of dawn, when the neon lights of rue Bréa and rue Vavin go out, this little restaurant-bar suddenly comes to life (it leads into *la Villa.*) Closing time about 8 a.m.

Saint-Michel/Mouffetard

L'Atelier de Maitre Albert 1, rue Maître-Albert, 633-13-78.

Receives you by candlelight, but the marvelous beams of this studio turned restaurant (specializing in hors d'oeuvres and grilled meats) are lit by projectors. Soothed by the sound of classical music, you could forget that the menu is meager. Nothing is more boring than tables with unimaginative hors d'oeuvres, nor is anything more irritating than a choice between "entrecôtes" (rib steaks), "brochettes" (meat grilled on a skewer), and "côtes d'agneau" (ribs of lamb).

Come with a dieting date—she will be happy with the menu and love the atmosphere—and watch out for the high-priced wine list, it will sky-rocket your check. (Closed on Sunday)

Le Coupe-Choux. 9, rue de Lanneau, 633-68-69.

Serves late enough to permit you to sup on "aubergines et oeufs en poelons" (eggplant and eggs in the pan), "grillades aux herbes" (grilled meat with herbs) or "bourguignon" (beef with glazed onions, mushrooms & wine).

It is a charming and sophisticated restaurant managed by young comedians: within a few years it expanded enough to occupy a whole building. Since one of the actor-restaurant-keepers is a cousin of Edgar Pisani, you will find at the *Coupe-Choux* a wine produced on the Minister's estate, Chateau Targé. Edwige Feuillère, Marie Daems, Soraya, Bernard Buffet and Annabel are among their elegant clientele. The menu lacks volume and you will pass the 35-franc mark as a result of the establishment's growing pains. (Closed in August)

La Truffière. 4, rue Vlainville, 633-29-82.

Justifies its name. Like all good Perigourdins (from Périgord), the owners know everything about truffles and convey their fine taste to a clientele of lawyers, doctors and movie stars (the Brasseurs, father and son, Marie-Joseé Nat and Jacques Charrier have been converted to cooking comme à Sarlat).

Good home-made "foie-gras," "cèpes du Périgord" (flap mushrooms from Périgord) preserved but not bleached to retain their scent, "confit d'oie et de canard" (goose and duck meat preserved in fat) and a gentle vin de Cahors. All this in addition to the dramatic ceiling-beams the air-conditioning and the hearty welcome justifies the check of 60 F. (at least). The prices are much too close to the ones at *le Grand Véfour,* but this restaurant is worth it. You can hang around till 2 in the morning, but the last orders are taken at 12:30 (reservations are preferable). (Closed on Sunday)

La Bucherie. 41, rue de la Bûcherie, 033-24-52.

Keeps its two wood-decked halls open every night till 2 a.m. Discreetly lit fireplace and classical background music give this place an air of a pleasant and calm mountain lodge. Nothing to single out on the menu. Tables too narrow, and a check for about 25 francs.

le Cheval Vert. 25, rue Descartes, 633-50-11.

At midnight it still serves chachlik and blinis. In this little restaurant, twin to the cabaret *le Cheval d'Or,* you can even do your shopping. The owner has an adjoining take-along cellar. Estimate 20 to 30 francs for a pleasant Russian-style meal.

Félix. 23, rue Mouffetard, 707-68-78.

Serves till very late, approximately 25 francs, but you may have just a drink at the bar (3.50 F.). It is generally quiet, except when show-business youngsters come to eat en masse!

Restaurants

Gargamelle. 5, rue de Pontoise, 326-56-81.
Offers till 1:30 a good full meal for 30 francs: copious hors d'oeuvres, steaks grilled in the back of the room on a large hearth, wine of Corbière stocked by the barrel, light and classical background music. The pianist, Errol Garner, patronizes the place when he comes to Paris. So do members of les Compagnons de la Chanson and some others. (Closed on Sunday in Summer)

le Grand Pavois. 8, rue Boutebrie, 633-86-24.
Has two surprises for you: a charming false patio (where the ceiling is a trompe-l'oeil giving the illusion of the night sky of Midi) and a miniature Saint-Tropez harbor where you dine in boats that will never sail. This honest and well-decorated restaurant serves till 1 a.m. and offers a third surprise: even if you ignore the fixed-meals priced at 16 to 20 francs, you can hardly go higher than 30 francs. (Closed on Sunday)

La Montagne Pelée. 13, rue Tournefort, 707-01-39.
Serves its "accras" (deep fried potato concoction), its "boudin antillais" (West Indian black pudding), its "crabe farci" (stuffed crab), and three guitarists from the West Indies, till 2 in the morning, sometimes later.

For 30 francs, and for those who love the taste of rum, it is charming and just dandy.

Le Mouff 5. 5, rue Mouffetard, 033-97-33.
Will amuse non-Parisians. This grocery-restaurant-bar for students and beatnicks doesn't lack quaintness. You could possibly eat there on an evening of broke solitude, but we advice you not to bring an elegant or over-25 girl friend with you.

La Raclette. 8, rue Suger, 633-13-26.
Fortunately stays open till a very late hour. Due to the slowness of the service, you can't just make a brief stop there.

The "tripes fertoises en brochette" (tripes on skewer, as in La Ferté) are less mysterious than you might think and hardly worth the trouble. The same goes for the "raclette valaisienne" (fondue with cheese from Valais) served with potatoes, and the "côtes de veau pop'art" (ribs of veal), which isn't at all psychedelic (since the place likes bizarre qualifications).

The door of *la Raclette* is just high enough to let Pietral the midget through, the decor is rustic and the check reasonable—20 to 25 francs.

Le Requin Chagrin. Place de la Contrescarpe, corner of rue Mouffetard, 033-18-87.

Lights its old beams with candles and offers you "boudin" (black pudding) an "riz créole" (rice cooked in a way to maintain its firmness), fish and "haricots rouges" (kidney beans). It is spicy and it seems West Indian, but it really is Reunion-style (Reunion is an island off the eastern coast of Africa) cooking. Calm and elegant clientele, check of 20 to 25 francs, open till two o'clock. A small bar-discotheque in the basement. (Closed on Monday)

AND MORE . . .

You can also have supper or a late dinner in *les Drugstores,* in *les Wimpy* (only if you are alone and "under the weather"), and in most of the bars mentioned in the preceding chapter.

A few discotheques can quiet the hunger pangs of the early-morning famished dancers. Such is the case with *le Bilboquet, le Birdland, le Carnaby, le Mini-Metro, le Play-Boy, le Pousse-au-crime, le Stardust* and *le Tournefort.*

This is not to mention the cabarets with supper-shows nor dozens of "excellent restaurants" we forgot to mention, nor hundreds of snack-brasseries and "troquets" (pubs) generally frequented by milkmen, road-sweepers and night watchmen.

CLUBS AND DISCOTHEQUES

Don't look for the word "discotheque" in your French-English dictionary, it probably isn't there. Don't worry about the legal definition of the word "club," it will get you nowhere.

Better lend an ear to a discotheque haunter, a confirmed insomniac who has been dragging his dark glasses for the past 15 years in sleepless nights, asking nothing more than to talk. When his victims cannot muster up enough courage to take leave, he goes on until the alcoholic dawn. A strict adherent to mother insomnia, he is at his best at midnight and drinks daily his ten glasses of 86 proof alcohol, but can bear neither the aperitifs nor the intoxication of others. This doesn't prevent him from having exceptional affairs with girls of quality or even pick-ups after everybody else has gone to sleep. There is a bottle kept in his name in five discotheques and he is on friendly terms with the management. Coquettishly he wears a polo shirt where the attendant prefers ties. He knows the club owners, their friends and associates, the personnel, a fair number of regular customers and all the strangers who intercept him. But on Saturday he pretends knowing no one.

Thanks to the fresh night air of Deauville, Cannes and Saint-Tropez, he maintains his health and manages to work for a living. He organizes his schedule in such a way as to live at night and still sleep a little, though he answers the phone at 11 a.m. This man knows all there is to know about the fabled dolce vita at these marvelous clubs. We give him the floor. . . .

During the era of the twist, night folk were going to bed at about 6 or 7 p.m. Today it is 4 a.m.; or 3 a.m. when they have a breakfast appointment. When they are really drained of energy, they leave with the "normal" clientele—at 2 in the morning.

They officially wake up at about 10 a.m. But their soul-and-conscience doesn't till after strong coffee and a few phone calls, which is by noon. Then they don't necessarily go on a sleeping binge. . . .

Depressions are for people who work too much and suffer everyday worries. They are for girls too. A nocturn recovers very well from his nightly rovings when he quits for health, work or love reasons. But women don't fare well in the night and cannot kick the habit without a solid masculine helping hand. Women feel free just because they hop till dawn from one man to the next, but it all ends in disaster when they don't let go on time. Alcohol, night living and love at dawn make them old prematurely.

In nocturnal circles you take a drink like someone else might smoke a cigaret. It is a gesture, a habit. Whiskey and soda for six months, bourbon for the next six, then gin-fizz, followed by screwdrivers and then back to whisky and soda. Some beer or a drop of Dom Pérignon may be consumed, but habitués prefer owning their own bottle. It is always within reach, and it doesn't disturb the personnel. . . . Alcohol keeps you awake.

When you finally drive home in safe second gear, only to be hit by a reveller who drank more than you and was zooming about in fourth, you may regret that you stayed out so late. You could also feel sorry for yourself, when you drive your companion home as dawn flickers: you glance at her mussed make-up and get sick. . . .

At the start, you have great fun at night and you proclaim it everywhere. Later it all depends on your friends and the girls you meet. At times you may be bored, but hardened insomniacs don't mind it.

Night-owls chat, do some girl-watching, make the round of the joints, proceed systematically to get intoxicated or to simply gape at nothing. You may build up a line of intelligent or funny conversation, or merely comment on the arrival of a ravishing beauty on the arm of an unappealing man. If you can stand it, try dancing the jerk or join a discussion on Vietnam. A discotheque is like a Spanish inn. There is the decor and the personality of the maître-de-maison, but you must rely mostly on yourself and the habitués for a good time.

People who go out once a week or once a month find discotheques and clubs great fun, if they aren't driven away by the noise, the mob and the heat. It is like a Zoo, with lots of pretty girls, bottles of scotch everywhere, stars out to be seen or playing a poor incognito game, and the little jerk dancers in a trance. . . .

Old club haunters dance the slows only to find out what a timid girlfriend thinks. Male night-prowlers who have passed the threshold of 30 don't jerk. They leave it to girls who dance among themselves or with minets.

In order to get there, you must obtain admission to the so-called private clubs, which is feasible if you find it agreeable that a drink may cost 18 to 22 francs and a bottle 160 to 200 francs. You also have to expect to waste some time.

The best way to come in would be with a habitué who can plead the cause of a neophyte. Otherwise, you can drop in around midnight and tell the checkroom girl that you have an appointment with someone-famous-who-is-about-to-join-you (name a star currently appearing at the Olympia, or any rock singer, or the most talked about person in the gossip columns).

Sober elegance is vital on this first contact. Do not lose your cool when you are sternly stared at through a peep-hole, admit that you are not known, and give the impression that you will behave properly. You can try to sneak in with a group of loyal customers who have entrée, but this is rather risky.

If you are audacious, try pretending that you have an appointment with the owner. But try it on a Saturday night only when the girl is so overworked that she has no time to confirm it. (Don't imagine that it will be necessarily work with Régine's, Castel, François-Patrice, or Minski.)

Once inside, sit at the bar; order a bottle. Don't just hang around stupidly (it irritates the habitués). Don't show that you are out of place by staying too long. Better go out casually, leaving behind decent tips for the barmen and hat-girl. If you have chosen the "date with a celebrity approach," say nonchalantly to the lady at the door, "What a pity that Johnny (Hallyday), Enrico (Macia), Claude (François) or Richard (Anthony) didn't show up. When you see him would you tell him please how long I waited."

The only risk you run is that of bumping into the other party at the door, but he will hopefully think he knows you from somewhere and will give you a friendly tap on the back when you reproach him for coming so late, just when you have to leave.

Two or three days later, you may come back and find the door slammed in your face. You must adopt a pleasantly hurt air and say, "Decidedly, you never recognize me! After all, I have a bottle here!" Next, you only need learn the first names of the barman and waiters or get acquainted with the girl who knows someone who knows the manager or the owner. Now you are a habitué, one of those who complain that they see too many new faces around.

When you own one club's key you can easily find the sesame that opens the doors to the other ones, unless you have the look of an escaped convict. The rest is easy, you just drink a lot, address one and all with the familiar "tu" and invite everybody until you feel totally at ease. If you repeat over and over again a few of the original truths found in this guide . . . and announce loudly that the discotheque era is washed out, you will sound like any long-time member.

You will be a full-fledged member all year except on New Year's Eve when they refuse to take out your bottle. Instead of coming to the club with hands full of presents, night-owls have taken to the custom of celebrating St. Sylvester by requesting that the management overvalue their personal checks.

Rive Gauche (Left Bank)

Le Bilboquet. 13, rue Saint-Benoît, 222-51-09.
Rallies the "Gros Minets" from old Saint-Germain and the "petits minets" dressed by Mayfair and the Renoma brothers, card players and jerk dancers. It is a bar a restaurant and a club.

The uncertainties of Germano-pratin cooking are particularly sensitive to the galerie-restaurant that circles the club (soberly decorated by Christian Girard), but you can safely dine on a neo-chinese entrée and the plat-du-jour, usually well-prepared (estimate 35 francs per person, with the house wine). In any case, one doesn't come to *le Bilboquet* to carefully choose some delicacy but to get together with friends or to feel at home during the hours separating the aperitif from midnight flirts. On quiet days, you can even take a shot at the bilboquet game (cup-and-ball), guided by the personnel.

The bar, in British style, is comfortable (drinks are 5 to 10 F.) slightly higher when an orchestra joins the excellent Bob Martin). Despite parking difficulties, it is the number one meeting place on Saint-Germain des-Prés, if one doesn't dine chez *Castel* or *King*. The atmosphere varies with each day, but the ex-singing waiter, Raoul Saint-Yves, carries out his functions as night-entertainment-adviser (a title he invented, which gives him carte blanche) with pleasant and carefree lazyness.

Maurice Casanova and Roland di Borgo, owners of the *Bilboquet,* usually dine at one of the tables juxtaposing the entrance —these and the ones on the small summer terrace are in greatest demand. The two owners occasionally dine in the basement where the former *Club Saint-Germain* is presently being revived. After a few years of only go-go music, the steady customers on rue Saint-Benoît are returning to their former loves. To swing orchestras and New Orleans jazz "improved" and adapted.

Chez Castel. 14, rue Princesse, 326-90-22.
They could turn back a "P.D.G." (president of a company) arriving with a high class call-girl in order to welcome a hippy-gigolo and his sulking girl friend. The only rule of the game is a friendly relationship with Jean Castel, and Huguette, a

"portière," whose absolute powers are deceptively concealed in her booth.

In the bar, the sullen goldfish couldn't care less about the records, though they are masterfully programmed by the best disc-jockey in Paris. So effective is he, that you cannot keep away from the dance floor for more than an hour. Especially if you were able to get a great table by the dance floor.

Refreshments are 20 francs with a side order of coca-cola served in the familiar bottle which the waiter delicately removes from the table. The minettes in transe are beautiful and not really stupid, but after Dutronc, everybody knows all about the girls from *Chez Castel.* The young dancers who invade the basement belong to a third undetermined sex, but the members of the *Castel*-gang, who get intoxicated at the three ground-floor tables, emanate solid masculinity. They are in their thirties and more often in their forties, and they spend their time getting drunk among old Saint-Germain-des-Prés friends. They have enough presence of mind to act drunk only when playing the old rascals. They love the night like no "yé-yé" who invaded rue St-Benoît can. They all are good friends of Castel, since *l'Epi-Club;* he is one night club owner who isn't obsessed by business profits.

Among the old-timers, you find honorable representatives of show-business: Antoine, François Hardy, Jacques Dutronc, Johnny Hallyday and Richard Anthony; the Deffe brothers and Grégoire Katz, the best Jewish story-teller in Paris. This intimate little circle usually dines in the first floor restaurant.

Le Francois-Patrice Saint-Hilaire. 24, rue Vavin, 033-90-95.

François-Patrice, who likes to keep the Parisians in step, introduced the hully-gully, the tamouré, the sirtaki and the let-kiss on rue de Ponthieu. He celebrated his first anniversary in Montparnasse by introducing the "casatchoc" imported from Russia, but Frenchified and tempered with a little jerk.

François-Patrice's new discotheque was decorated by Christian Gérard and installed on the premises of the old *Eléphant Blanc,* enlarged for the occasion through annexation of the terrace and the cellars. The exposed metal framework, the staggered levels and the gangway towering over the dance floor belong to modernism as it was conceived in the days of Gustave Eiffel. But the complicated plan of the polished-steel bar, the projectors, and the air conditioning system belong to the era of astronauts. The British juke-box of the new *Saint-Hilarie* is installed on a freight elevator and is visible to clients seated on the rising levels of the club itself. But it has no access to the upper floor, the latter being reserved for eating and soft music.

While the discotheque is conventionally reserved for the jerk and whiskey lovers (20 francs the drink, 200 the bottle), dinner and supper are far from traditional at the restaurant, open from 7 p.m. till dawn (see chapter on restaurants).

Roger Urbini was supposed to direct it on his return from *l'Esquinade* at Mégève, his twin brother held the fort in the meantime. François-Patrice kept the whole crew from the *Saint-Hilaire* of rue de Ponthieu (which became a cabaret six months later) including the "savoyard" (Savoie native) barman. The old crew helps to acclimatize the clientele, faithful since the days of *la Tortue* and the first *Licorne,* to the left bank. Only King Hussein of Jordan has failed to turn up, he was deprived night life as well as of one part of Jordan.

François-Patrice, who is associated with Gérard Perrault, doesn't rest on his laurels just because he can count on the loyalty of the Duke of Windsor, Marléne Dietrich, Gilbert Bécaud, Robert Hossein, Jean Marais and Johnny Hallyday. While trying to keep Christian Girard's hydraulic ashtrays working (they have the unfortunate tendency to leak, overflow or clog), he has started to install a garden-terrace over the restaurant. In summer, supper will be served over the little square, that tiny island of greenery at the crossroads of two neon-and-cabaret-decked streets. Considering that *le Saint-Hilaire* is reserved for François-Patrice's friends and his friends' friends, it is wise to go there sponsored by a "friend" if you don't know the blond Coraline, a charming but strict Cerberus.

Le King-Club. 17, rue de l'Echaudé, 633-00-24.
Is the most comfortable of the large classic discotheques. After a weak but financially sound début, Albert and Maxime Minski's club found its cruising speed and its style. A calm and anonymous basic clientele brilliant young actors such as Michel Duchaussoy and a group of singers trained by Johnny Hallyday, Richard Anthony and Claude-François.

Newly arrived to night life in 1961, with the opening of his *King,* Albert Minski's great merit lies in the fact that he was able to assert himself by promoting comfort and quality. In his night Parisians have discovered the charms of soft benches, efficient air-conditioning and a good sound system, as well as the first podium for "command girls" in ultra short skirts.

Even though *King* didn't have as resounding a début as the fashionable spots of the twist era, you might meet there Brigitte Bardot, Liz Taylor or Richard Burton, whose presence Minski regretfully, or tastefully, didn't exploit. He learned to use the publicity of gossip columns, but never forgot the essentials. His club looks as new today as on its opening day.

We won't dwell longer on this discotheque that turned the comfortable habits of night-owls upside down. You may read more about King—now a real night-complex—in the chapter on restaurants. Before we make an appointment with you at the second floor bar or in the billiard room, we would like to remind you that Micheline watches the entrance rather strictly, and that a scotch is 20 francs.

Le New Jimmy's. 124, bd du Montparnasse, 326-74-14.
Is Régine's, and we won't try to explain Régine to those unfortunate night-owls who have gone mad trying to force her door, equipped with a spy-hole and jealously guarded. We admit that she isn't svelte, that she does happen to drink as much at times as her customers and that she may not be able to refrain from talking too frankly. But we know that she is betrothed to the night, that she doesn't lack acumen, and that she is extremely hard-working. This book deals only with nightly activities and inactivities, yet we would like to tell you that the interpreter of "Petits Papiers" wakes up quite early after her wakeful nights to lead a professional career by day as a singer.

"Gueule de nuit" (a nickname given to her by Barbara who dedicated a song to her) likes black and decorated her club in super-black, with electrical garlands (installed on the ceiling—New Year's 1968) throwing psychedelic lights. Like the motorman of an old locomotive, the disc-jockey has to bend out of his cabin to watch the dance floor. His eyes by now accustomed to darkness, he plays the right proportion of wild and slow records (including a few of Régine's songs) according to the degree of agitation in the room.

François Sagan, Jacques Chazot, Jean Cau, Gilbert Bécaud, Georges Cravenne, Otto Preminger and Sammy Davis Jr.—when they are in Paris—form the honor guard of "la Grosse" (to them the adjective isn't pejorative) and keep watch at the entrance. The three tables where Tout-Paris walks by and doesn't always dare linger, are Régine's personal fief. She joins her most loyal friends there, between trips to the dance floor of the bar.

Brigitte Bardot, who matches her hair to the place by wearing her dark wig on incognito nights, prefers the table near the narrow passage to the bar. Accompanied by Gunther Sachs, Serge Gainsbourgh or her gang, she cares little about the price: 22 francs the drink, 200 the bottle of scotch. Anonymous clients are only too delighted to be charged the same prices as the super-stars.

A small room in the basement gives you a chance to talk without having to shout, but you won't see there the beautiful and sophisticated girls who come to the *New Jimmy's* with their upper class flirt, their father or a contemporary of their father's. Minets in fitted jackets using their daddy's Jaguar and bottle try to take airs of old revellers at the bar. When they are gone, Régine often improvises a dawn spaghetti-party, free and reserved for the more persistent of her friends, those who can go without blinking an eye from the absolute darkness of *Jimmy's* to the pale but natural light of boulevard Montparnasse and its first traffic. . . .

Le Black Jack. 33, rue Vavin, 326-78-98.
Abandoning the idea of a cabaret, André Farry gave this place over to Lotte Castel, ex-wife of Jean, who managed the *Epi-Club* with her husband, from 1957 to 1962. The decor with pleasant saloon woodwork hasn't changed, but it now a discotheque where the clients of local cabarets gladly stop for a last drink during hours when strip-teasers put their clothes back on. It was Jean Castel who offered his former wife the posters that decorate the place. Scotch is 15 francs at the bar, 20 francs at a table; Champagne starts at 130 francs, service included.

Le Carnaby. 10, rue Servadoni, 326-99-42.
Really looks like a club—and not because of a laxer doorman than at Régine's. You can chat here in real easy-chairs, read the paper or dream of the passing nights without being jostled by the personnel and customers. The place is quiet and tastefully furnished, pleasantly anonymous. After watching some television, you can dine. But if you feel like moving around, you can go down to the attractive discotheque in the basement.

Le Cherry Lane. 8, rue des Ciseaux, 326-28-28.
Has a clientele of charming and not too well-behaved minets, who do the jerk in a black laquered decor and have no plans to re-make the world. Refreshments are 5 to 10 francs. There are plenty of young girls about. (Closed on Sunday)

Le Club Rive Gauche. 11, rue Bernard-Palissy, 222-51-70 and 51-71.
Is managed by Touré who set up shop between its four walls after leaving *le King-Club*. This native of New-Guinea, who knows Paris better than Conakry—he started in 1947—receives P.D.G.'s (company presidents), rich and quiet strangers, cinema folk. It isn't madly "go-go" but service is quite adequate (20 francs the shot, 190 and 220 francs the bottle of scotch) and the atmosphere pleasantly bizarre.

Touré doesn't play the club game excessively. He receives friends of his friends first, but he also welcomes strangers who know how to introduce themselves and behave well (most of the other joints do as much but don't admit it).

As a result of defective sound-proofing, Touré had to amputate the little balcony over the main room in order to lower the ceiling. In its stead, he shortened the bar and reserved a corner for those who wish to chat without being deafened by the records of Petit-Touré (the disc-jockey, no relation). The club is run well and the air-conditioning effective.

Le Club des Saints-Pères. 10, rue des Saint-Pères, 222-16-33, 548-71-61.
Was set up by Jean Vergnes in the beautiful caves of Don Camillo. After a shaky start, the place now has a regular turnover during the week and crowds on Friday and Saturday. An anonymous and respectable clientele, an appreciable crew of pretty girls and some singers—some preferring the first floor and some dining on the ground floor, where Brigitte Bardot and Gina Lollobrigida have been seen. Dinner for roughly 25 francs.

Jean Vergnes, whom you will recognize by the dark glasses and his discretion, does not keep his doors closed like Régine and Castel. But you can't just walk in casually. Let us say that you can penetrate the place without pull, but you must know how to present yourself and do it well. A bottle of scotch is 200 francs and one shot is 22 francs. (see *Don Camillo* in the chapter on supper shows)

Le Greenwich Village. 10, rue Descartes, 033-50-96.
Faces the Ecole Polytechnique, but flirting there is discreet without special equations for love. The doors open without recommendation but they are closed to "dragueurs" (wolves)—there is also no bar there which makes it quite unbearable to men alone. It is a charming and calm spot where you can hesitate between a small room and a miniature cellar. Whiskey is 15 francs the shot and 120 francs the bottle.

Le Jacky's Farwest Saloon. 11, rue Jules-Chaplain, 033-68-87.
Is a discotheque for youngsters who do a quiet jerk and don't act like cowboys. It seems harmless enough in a neighborhood full of cabarets and clubs for de-luxe squares ("croûlants"). Cover charge and a drink cost a modest 6 francs during the week, 8 F. on Friday, and 10 F. on Saturday.

Le Mini-Metro. 6, rue des Ciseaux, 326-33-31.
Fills up from the overflow of the *Cherry Lane,* unless it is the other way around. Pretty minets with pretty faces, a few rare minettes who fortunately are not prejudiced. The cellar sometimes features an orchestra. The ground floor is a restaurant (a meal is 12 francs).

Le Pousse au Crime. 15, rue Guisarde, 633-36-63.
May send your girl-friend into the arms of a "garçonne" (lesbian in male rôle). This quiet little discotheque is women's territory, but men are welcome to have a drink or buy a bottle (the latter 150 F.). We met Darryl Zanuck and Robert Hossein there. Some of the clients, beautiful and young, are not insensitive to masculine charm. You could invite them to dine with you very late, in the ground floor restaurant.

Service is nice and the seating uncomfortable. It is a club but a membership card is not indispensible. An introduction by one of Yvonne's friends will suffice. Formerly of *Carroll's,* she now owns *le Pousse au Crime.* (Closed on Sunday)

La Question. 1, rue Frédéric-Sauton, 033-73-06.
Is known only to night-rovers who don't get around much and take up quarters by Boul'Mich. It is a labyrinth of old caves where you can listen to records without worrying about what is happening at *Castel.* Refreshments are 15 francs.

Le Ruby's Club. 31, rue Dauphine, 633-68-16.
Is as comfortable as *le King* and as pleasantly decorated too. Set up at great cost in an old potato warehouse, the joint was endowed with an extraordinary ceiling of hammered copper, assembled with oriental patience by artisans from Beyruth. The music is well proportioned but the disc-jockey could raise the volume as high as it can go since the club was taken apart two months after it opened, as a result of neighbors' complaints of noise, and then totally sound-proofed.

Leila Jazy—of Lebanese and Sicilian origin—who was Miss Tunis before she immersed herself in the Parisian night, is a remarkably sleepless hostess. Before she came to *Ruby's,* this former student of chemistry learned from Régine all the secret formulas of the night. By working as door-keeper at *New Jimmy's* she got to know the after-midnight clientele.

Until the summer of '68 the door at *Ruby's* was watched by the debonnaire Fifi Baheux, whose heart gave up one dawn, after 30 years of burning the candle at both ends. He had refused to listen to his doctor; a diurnal man could not influence this "old night-rascal," who had his debut at *Liberty's.*

A drink runs 18 francs and a bottle 180 francs in this joint where the time of night is easily forgotten. Loving "tête-à-têtes" inspired by the decor and the discreet atmosphere break up very late.

Le Speakeasy. 4, rue les Canettes, 326-83-77.
Has a very masculine clientele, apparently indifferent to fem-

inine wiles. We met there a few minets behaving quite properly but obviously wearing the heart of a "minette". Women, who are admitted here, will appreciate the cushioned quietness of this well-kept little place but won't exactly find romance.

Le Stardust. 10, rue Guenegaud, 033-98-56.
Has been the rallying place for club disc-jockeys, barmen, dancers and late stragglers. They are served rather nondescript food at hours where nobody cares about gastronomy. At the start it was relatively enjoyable but it has lost its freshness. One last dive into the lower-level discotheque gave us a chance to admire the barman's handiness. For a full 20 minutes we watched him collect left-over coca-cola without wasting a single drop. The latest news: they plan to restart. We shall see.

Le Tabou. 33, rue Dauphone, 633-33-95.
In the days of Boris Vian and the great Paroissiens, this was one of the highlights of Saint-Germain-des-Prés. Now, for 6 to 9 francs on weekdays and 10 or 12 F. on Saturdays, the "yé-yés" swing there. They wear their hair as long as the existentialists of yesteryear, but the resemblance stops there. . . .

Other discotheques:

—le Baldaquin. 13, rue Mazarin, 033-58-84.
—le Birdland. (see chapter on jazz).
—la Bohême. 16, rue d'Odessa, 326-60-77.
—le Cardinal. 74, Card.—Lemoine, 633-01-21.
—le Club Vénitien. 27, rue de Buci, 633-62-09.
—le Fiacre. (see chapter on restaurants).
—la Niche aux Cabots. 3, rue crébillion, 326-32-46.
—la Paillotte. (see chapter on jazz).
—le Requin Chagrin. (see chapter on restaurants).
—le Riverboat. 67, r. St-André-des-Arts.
—le Roméo. 71, bd St-Germain, 033-07-76.
—la Tour de Nesle. 6, rue de Nesle, 633-03-09.
—le Tournefort. 7, rue Tournefort, 535-43-10.

Rive Droite (Right Bank)

Le Club de l'Etoile. 4, avenue Victor-Hugo, 727-69-46.
Was created by Paul Pacini in the 60's, when the twist rage was coming on strong. After mad nights animated by beautiful

young women, the place suffered a set-back when the discreet and charming Charlie Bogey had a short tour at *Twenty One* and then at *King*. After finally returning to the fold, this svelte old night-stager, straightened everything out and recuperated the XVIe arrondissement's golden youths, who were being lured to Saint-Germain-des-Prés.

It is a discotheque, judging by the records played there. Nevertheless, it exploits fully the orchestra game. Anglo-Saxon groups, noisy but good, stir up the young clientele every evening (except on Saturdays). Charlie Bogey carefully limits their "sets" so that his quadrogenarian clients don't start dreaming of "boules de Quies" (ninepins). We are so used to the decor that we cannot effectively comment upon it, but on more lucid nights, we find it neutral and scanty.

If you are accompanied by a lady who wants to see and be seen, take a table in the main room. But if you would rather chat, a seat at the bar is more appropriate. Service is courteous, a shot of whiskey is 20 francs and a bottle 200 F.

A detail to remember when you are turning back home through the somber depths of the XVIe arr. of Neuilly and wonder where to stop for a night cap: *l'Etoile* is the only islet of light after the Arce de Triomphe.

Le Psychédélic. 12, rue de Ponthieu, 225-51-70.
A local boy established this night spot as an original and ultramodern electronic innovation in decor; and it made a big hit at first. However, after the initial novelty wore off, the vogue of the *Psychédélic* soon ended and the club has closed "pour transformations," in preparation for a new edition.

Le Carroll's Club. 12, rue Sainte-Anne, 742-97-86.
Receives the girl friends and entourage of the famous Frède—who brought together Tout-Paris at *Carroll's*, when Annabel was still singing and before she married Bernard Buffet. The discotheque on rue Sainte-Anne is less wonderous than the former, but you can stare at pretty girls there who, despite their obvious fancy for females, are not always intractable to males. Frède was quite ill as we penned these lines. We hope health returns quickly.

Les Chadelles 1, rue Pierre-le-Grand, 227-45-11
Is managed by a Breton who recreates in the summer the beautiful nights of Trebeurden. Yves-de-Chandelles (they all call him so in the little circle of night-professionals) keeps the club open till 2 a.m. on weekdays and 4 a.m. on Saturdays. A drink is 12 francs, and a bottle is 150 F. The girls are delightful and sometimes—at the end of the week—they are alone.

Le Pierre-Charron. 52, rue Pierre-Charron, 359-35-30.
Set up quarters in a spacious basement with an interesting past. In the days of Django, it entertained le Hot Club de France, and the guitarists of La Puerta del Sol. Before the war, Edith Piaf sang in these beautiful caves and in 1938 she had been involved right here in a gloomy murder case.

Raymond Mamoudi—who wrote "l'Amour" for Mireille Mathieu and "Ailleurs qu'a Paris" for Dean Martin—has been managing the place for the past four years without interrupting his career in music publishing. People from the music hall and song world, such as Fernand Raynaud or François Deguelt, come in regularly. Pretty girls make the scene too. Refreshments are 14 francs the shot. Admittance is not so difficult until 5 a.m. Jam sessions; a Livre de Poche library for the obsessive reader!

La Plantation. 45, rue de Monpensier, 742-48-11.
Was begun in 1960 by Michael Nebot in quarters occupied by the Club des Planteurs during the revolution.

Although more whiskey is consumed there than punch, it still is one of the most colorful discotheques in Paris, where the cha-cha and the meringue are still danced as much as the jerk. African and West Indian girls move their hips with an agility to make the little blonde jerkers green with envy. Friendly and relaxed atmosphere, pretty girls of all races, formal and improvised entertainment. Drinks are 15 francs each and a bottle of whiskey is 170 francs.

Le Tekki. 125, rue de Sèvres, 556-97-13, 734-13-57.
Is the newest of the Parisian night-complexes. *Le Tekki* was opened by Jean Fradel in the vast quarters of a plushy and luxurious club, where amateurs of Japanese martial arts compete during the day. Before the opening of the discotheque and its annexes, the *Tekki* was known mostly to karate fanatics.

Since "black belts" go to sleep with the fall of night, Jean Fradel, conceived of the idea to train the abdomens of his nocturnal friends after the gym's closing hours. The sauna stays open for you to relax in after dancing the jerk all night. And to help keep insomniacs in shape, the large pool on the second floor will stay open too.

Hunger usually follows swimming and dancing, and Jean has provided an all night restaurant to serve supper (even vegetarian) to the famished guests. Finally for a relaxed digestion, enjoy the ultra-violet filtered light of the solarium adjoining the club. A drink 20 francs; a bottle of scotch 200 francs.

Le Whiskey a Gogo. 18, rue du Beaujolais, 742-75-43.

Is managed by a young Centralien, Alain Bensimon, but you may still see Paul Pacini, who opened the club in 1950 on the premises of the former *Plancher des Vaches*. When his only competition was Jean-Claude Merle's *la Discotheque*.

On the ground floor a quiet little bar in vague British style. On the lower level, a room with nooks and corners. The place has not changed since the heroic days of clubs. You mingle with journalists and young people. Prices are moderate as far as discotheques go: 120 the bottle of scotch, 12 francs the drink and 8 francs for a refill.

Other discotheques:

— le Bus Palladium. 6, rue Fontaine, 874-54-99.
— le César. 4, rue Chabanais, 742-41-79.
— le Cintra. (see chapter on bars).
— le Club Ecossais. 4, rue Jean Mermoz, 359-20-38.
— le Club Rive Droite. 33, rue Petits-Champs, 742-29-53.
— le Club Sainte-Anne. 7, rue Sainte-Anne, 742-83-99.
— la Dinanderie. (see chapter on restaurants).
— le Donkey. (see chapter on bars).
— le Gaslight. 41, rue du Colisée, 225-38-30.
— le Golf Drouot. 2, rue Drouot, 770-47-25.
— le Grill de la Plantation. (see chapter on restaurants).
— le Kiss Club Eldorado. 4, bd de Strasbourg, 208-45-12.
— le Milord Mod's. 5, rue Beaujolais, 236-88-14.
— le Tilbury. 9, rue Truffaut, 387-79-07.
— le Touquet. 1 bis, Jean-Mermoz, 359-18-40.
— le Tour Club. 8, rue de Tanger, 607-86-89.

"RATED X"

(for adults only)

Satan always leads the dance and he has even taken a liking to the jerk. Venal pleasures make up a sizable portion of the varigated Parisian night. The situation is not worse than in London, New York or Tokyo, nor is it more decadent today than in the days of Petrone and the libertine marquis. We would say "there is nothing to beat a dog about," if the expression didn't evoke some unhealthy impressions that belong in a treaty on sexology rather than in a guide.

We would like to escort you through the forbidden night as joyfully as we led you from restaurant to club, but we are not equipped to sell this book under the counter. Nevertheless, we shall be as precise as possible within limits. We will tell you enough that you might ask further information from barmen, "chasseurs," porters, "concierges d'hôtel" and taxi drivers without sounding ridiculous. They will advise you extensively.

God and Saint-Marthe may know why sexual fantasies and the minor curiosities of love are condemned more rigidly than excessive ingestion of alcohol or racing a 5 CV at top speed. There are always people who see Salmone and Mary-Magdalena as ladies of the Holy Spirit and fight vice, resulting only in making it change sidewalks. If we had a nasty disposition we would do homage to legislators who drive evil from the streets into hotels and force cathouses underground. All this complicates police work and compels interested customers to keep their little black books up to date. Police raids never result in reforming the "fille de joie" or homosexual minets. Just as microbes acquire new vigor after having resisted the first assault of antibiotics, immoral acts and the people who do them become attractive in clandestineness.

Since we are not qualified to give a scrupulous account of carnal acts committed out of wedlock (this book is not even illustrated), we will simply introduce you to the not-so-proper-types one might like to meet. They are:

★ Young girls who fend for themselves. Flowers in bloom, they don't always strike it rich, but they are desirable, everywhere and they don't consider themselves courtesans. Much fun.

★ Call-girls, invented by the modern world of P.T.T. (Post. Tel. & Tel.), are not listed in the yellow pages; just in the alphabetical listing.

★ Stay-at-home girls ("casanières"), who in the days of "Rachelle-qui-du-Seigneur" (from Halevy's opera) and the courtesans, would have inhabited a brothel. But no longer, after Marthe Richard and the post-World War II closings.

★ Perverse homosexuals. Normal homosexuality in Paris today is a mere diversion for bourgeois "Pater familias."

★ Transvestites, men turned sweet, often thanks to hormones and who sometimes stretch the fantasy so far as to become "lesbians."

★ Women's lady-loves.

We will only glance at the sidewalk which we prefer to leave to the hurried day-people. We would still have a weakness for some unclean Venus on Madeleine if it were not so embarrassing to be forced to park between two patrol cars stuffed with puritanical policemen. If any of our readers is attracted to the charms of the "macadam," we suggest he abandon the sidewalk for the roadway. The "amazones" (girls cruising in cars) have good brakes and an idea about what constitutes a worthwhile stop."

The Debutantes

Girls who fend for themselves don't defend their virtue, only their interests. These are young girls who may get into the habit of living off men without fully understanding that they are making their debut in prostitution—to the great displeasure of the "pros." Once they do understand their position, they feel no shame and merely organize more rationally the trade of their charms. Unless they get married in white to a lucky groom whose life they might only complicate. But that is none of our business!

Scattered in discotheques and constantly on the move, they get bored at *Maxim's,* dream of mini-skirts rather than furs, love minets and the jerk. They haven't yet stooped to running after their pigeons, but they do give in to gentlemen who could be their fathers without excessive displeasure. They won't think about the 100 francs for the coiffeur, or the check that comes on time for the rent. If you take one to Deauville for the weekend, don't give her much spending money. The good sea air should suffice.

Often minors, but highly developed sexually, these "easy" girls (which they are) have multiplied with the discotheques. Sometimes, bosses after having exploited their little teeny bopper bodies, don't pay them, which gives the "debutantes" a chance to jerk to their heart's desire before looking for a lonely client to cheer up. Adapted to the era of the Beatles and the respectability of night-spots, they perform as hostesses but don't get a cut from the house.

Night bachelors who don't gorge themselves with alcohol till their virility gives out, can choose between two tactics in dealing with these young girls:

★ If you are young, a good dancer, or well-spoken you can vie for the role of lover. It costs nothing, but requires a certain amount of patience. These little girls don't go to bed before dawn, sleep all day and besmear the sink with mascara. You may like this well enough, but you may also have to step aside every once in a while to free the bed for some other man, less handsome, but much richer. Tolerate brief gratuitous adventures with known singers and actors. These girls love to sample show-biz people and cannot see why others don't understand it.

★ If you are not-so-handsome-or-young, but cynical, worn out, impatient and rich, you can replace the lover for a few hours by making the lady a discreet contribution. A small monthly remittance will insure regular services until the girl becomes restless and looks for greener pastures.

Girls on their own admit only to rare friends and co-workers their reasons for not filing a tax return, so avoid putting your foot in your mouth by asking "how much?" Have yourself introduced to the girls by the owner, the host or the barman, let your new conquest jerk till she is breathless. Suggest going for a drink elsewhere—which makes you ungrateful to your cupid-host, but it makes you a good operator too. "Elsewhere," means another such noisy spot. Pretend to listen to your companion, who almost invariably will expose her financial worries, hint to a possible friendly arrangement and suggest another drink . . . this time at your place.

Prices in this field are not fixed, so try to average your own innate stinginess and the girl's hopes. Estimate 100 to 200 francs, and while paying, say, "I have no time to buy you the mini-skirt that would fit you so well (or the handbag, or the shoes, or the perfume). Choose it yourself." Pretend you believe her when she promises to reinburse you some day. For a bonus, she will tell you all about her provincial childhood, her disarray when faced with the big city and the high rents. This is the beginning of new negotiations, which you are not obligated to pursue.

It goes without saying that these young people will show candidness for only a year or two. You will meet them once again in this book, later in life, as call-girls, loyal boarders at a hotel kept by an old-fashioned "Madam," or "apartment girls" trading phone numbers of nice clients. Of course they may succeed in being sumptuously and regularly kept, much too bourgeois a situation (and too rare in these unpecuniary times) for us to bring up.

The Professionals

Girls who support themselves don't do so with a military obstinacy. Love interludes, virtuous crises, laziness, whims, and a vacation-craze prevent them from effectively commercializing their bodies. Professionals entertain a non-poetic clientele, seekers of venal pleasures. They work in more or less clandestine "clandés," in bars or through the telephone.

Prostitution is not illegal, but its promotion has been forbidden since 1946. Hence the closing of the "maisons Tellier." All has not been purified in the years following Marthe Richard. Private hotels and amiably open apartments—some managed by "madams" with good connections and a house in the country—are being revived without publicity or scandal, in the brothel tradition of yesteryear. On rue Paul-Valery, rue Rennequin, rue de Douai, rue Fonataine, rue de Léningrad, rue de la Pompe, and elsewhere it seems that one can find limited happiness on a schedule generally valued from 150 to 400 F, according to the taste and means of the client and the competence of the partner.

Since the madam takes half of the requested price, a tip should be highly appreciated by the "fiançée" who loses a half hour to an hour with a stranger. Give this little present (50 francs) before, to profit from the girl's good mood. Don't waste precious time making speeches to her. Girls know perfectly well they are "too beautiful, too well-bred, too intelligent to do that" and just relax during such sentimental homilies.

The strict managers of well-kept "clandés" censure all lascivious activity involving more than three partners. Although it is possible to commit bourgeois adultery in front of one's wife, or to ask for the company of two girls, wild bacchanales are proscribed.

There are places for these however, near boulevard des Batignoles, by place Pereire and rue de Chazelle. Only couples, licensed or libertine, are permitted there . . . all doors are open (cover charge, drink included, is 30 F. minimum. Afterwards—anything goes). If you don't want to risk your steady companion's virtue, you can request—for at least 200 F.—the assistance of a prostitute. It is somewhat embarrassing when you meet your doctor or dentist accompanied by their wives. Members of the medical profession, Englishmen in transit in Paris notably like societal carnality.

Multiple-partner athletes could find suitable couples on rue des Acacias as well, but we shall not develop this remarkable subject any further here. Nor will we dwell here upon the sado-masochistic specialty of some "clandés," sometimes closed down as a result of police raids.

Coming back to the pretty night merchants, we remind you that the young women who dream on a bar stool aren't always under the influence of alcohol. Tired of the hide and seek game with valiant police sergents (which ends with a 50 franc fine for girls and the loss of a night's work at their post) numerous street-walkers have abandoned the sidewalk for the quiet warmth of certain establishments. Especially in Pigalle, on the Champs-Elysées, and sometimes in Montparnasse, they wait for the merry night rabbits to whom they give a half hour of pleasure without love (50 to 100 F.) Though the demi-mondaines of eminent clandés are generally free of ties, a good many bar-girls are "married" and discreetly watched by their procurers. The owners close their eyes with interested tolerance. The girls are of age (usually), don't create a scandal, attract customers and leave the personnel large tips.

We don't wish to deprive our readers of the pleasures—or indignations—of discovering these bars (sometimes shut by the police or deprived of a night permit) all by themselves, we therefore suggest they stroll in cabaret neighborhoods and choose among the establishments with soft lights and blacked out windows. It is hard not to notice the girls and easy to perform instant-courting.

With the call-girls, we have arrived at the aristocracy of prostitution: mink stoles, good manners, a habit of big restaurants and big theatres, an almost fluent English. . . . Had they been born in the era of Christine Keeler, the courtesans of classic Greece would have undoubtedly started at the telephone, risen to be sumptuously kept, and finally declined. The classy call-girl submits with airs of a grand courtesan or a woman of the world, which justifies the price (100 to 300 francs for the "independents," 200 to 400 F. through a procuress, and 500 for an evening with dinner; nights and week-ends negotiable).

Call-girls start as "debutantes" then regularize their activities. Introduced to a Mme C. or B. (first name initials), they agree to stay by the phone from 2 p.m. to 2 a.m., ready for an invitation on short notice. If a docile and idle lover does not keep them company during the long waits when business is bad, they proceed to acquire some culture, beyond Guy de Cars, or simply to watch television. The procuress who lines up a contract for one of her fillies, sometimes insists on being paid in advance. The girls she trusts are paid directly by the client. They meet in the latter's home or more often in a cosy studio or discreet hotel. The amatory meeting is relatively short, a whiskey may be accepted or offered with a minimum of conversation. Trained call-girls don't like to waste their time and quickly respond to sensually excited gentlemen who want a "night," that they have to take care of their poodle or ailing old mother. At their next meeting with madam, they will give her half the sum received, in consideration for her good offices. Checks, travellers checks and most foreign currencies accepted.

Like a star leaving her too-greedy manager, the shrewder and more independent call-girls have a tendency to show ingratitude to the chaperones of their early days. Using psychology more than sexual prowess, they try to hold on to some of their partners and form a clientele they can keep in contact with directly without intermediary. It permits them to lower the price and earn still more money while keeping an eye out for an unhappily married wealthy gentleman who would keep them without bothering too much.

Deprived of the mercenary but efficient help of Madam, the independant girls sometimes find it hard to keep a clientele that is alas fickle and craves novelty. Rather than return repentant to the procuress—which often does happen—some girls create a combination. They pass their clients as gifts to friends who "send the ball back." Our uncouth editor would call it "a chicken pool" ("pool de poules").

Call-girls of bourgeois character and regularly falling in love with practical and nice enough young men, also rarely "visible," don't worry the police (some could be used for counter-espionage) and they are too uncontrollable to interest the classic procurer. This explains why they can get out of this business if they don't make a mess of their lives and their youth. Movie stars and even serious spouses of businessmen could testify to it if you could get them to reminisce their flighty years.

Between Boys

Homosexuals too can be victims of distressing impulses. Like normal men who flee kitchen love or slippers and T.V., they look for adventure in the night when they are bored at home. There are places, more or less discreet and not always distinguished, where they can hide an ancillary flirt with some Spanish valet, fall into the arms of a solid truckdriver or pass a moment with a minet with a heart of a minette.

Flitting about, more than any lady's man or lady's lady, amoral homosexuals often complain of the lack of variety in their nocturnal divertissements. Realizing that one cannot indefinitely vary his pleasures, we will establish that they have a choice between:

★ The open air: if business on rue du Colisée and avenue Gabriel is lax, les Tuileries and Champs-de-Mars are propitious for meetings, moneyed or otherwise. Homosexuals who don't hide their wallets before looking for soul mates will pay 50 to 150 F. for their brief interlude with a tender or muscular creature who might accost them at Saint-Germain-des-Prés. In Pigalle, one can find minets at bargain prices and a few old "tantes" (passive inverts) strolling along the streets. But nature lovers could meet evil connections at the Bois de Boulogne. Natives recommend allée de la Longue Quene.

★ Steam: the indispensable complement of sail for some night navigators, covers only partially the turbid and ephemeral loves born in bathing establishments that are too specialised for just grooming. (Usually open till midnight, sometimes till 2 a.m. on Saturday nights, propitious for popular loves. Door price, including a robe is 10 to 20 F.)

Those who dream nostalgically of San Francisco or the around-the-clock establishments with bar, restaurant, and "orgie room" found there, appreciate the soft music of a place near the Ternes. By Saint-Philippe-du-Roule, actors, now married, used to pamper their bodies tenderly (and mutually) when they were young and wild. But it seems that this has declined. Now having become fathers, like any heterosexual, they have apparently given up the pleasures of the sauna and the massage.

If you like serious people, and wish to jest with financial specialists who don't look like executives when their clothes are off, you must take in rue du Faubourg St-Honoré, two steps from rue des Pyramides. If you prefer to stay in the XVIe arr. with the genteel inverts, look around by avenue Victor-Hugo.

With a towel thrown over their arm as clothing, Adam plays up to Eve as well as possible in left bank establishments, blessed by Allah . . . but open to infidels. Admirers of ravishing workmen and graceful mechanics hide their weakness for the proletariate in the XVIIe arr. (the upstairs rooms are costlier, but a robe, a sponge and occasional visits to the popular lower level are included in the price.)

Despite careful screening at the door, a policeman occasionally manages to take his clothes off and then request the unnatural lovers to put theirs back on, and follow him to the station. Such visits generally end with a temporary closing of some health clubs with too exclusive a clientele.

★ Night clubs and restaurants: A few establishments also receive a normal, somewhat sympathetic or simply curious clientele. At *Ficare,* Louis is not shaken by the arrival of Baron de Charlus accompanied by a minet, but welcomes more courteously some sophisticated young ladies who don't take offense at their escort's short visits to the ground floor, where the clientele is exclusively masculine.

At *la Mangeoire* too, the sexes are mixed in the restaurant, while the lower level is more exclusive (at *le Blitis,* the feminine element is represented chiefly by a few lesbians who gladly leave the men to their own). The same tolerance of love in the masculine form is to be found at the *Speakeasy* and *chez Michou*, where women are received with "galanterie" often forgotten by normal men. *Le Petit Vendôme, le Prélude, le Vagabond* and *le César* are more exclusive. At *Primm's* it would be very ridiculous to come with wife or to make heterosexual proclamations on the staircase where queens crowd on good nights. Total and distinguished masculinity at *Club 13,* which receives a very Parisian clientele.

Homosexuals can also hide their love in numerous bars or whisper sweet nothings to their conquests in the green fields near Paris, where several establishments offer idyllic week-ends. As long as it isn't too obvious, the police prove rather tolerant, especially since closings and pestering leads only to the emigration of homosexuals to safer meeting grounds. The Mondaine nevertheless was severe enough in 1967, they withdrew authorization to stay open from 2 to 4 in the morning, and forced the very exhibitionistic couples to restrain themselves in public.

Since homosexuality itself is not outlawed, policemen only attack establishment owners who let minors in or who tolerate bolder flirts. Dancing among men is one of the prohibited pleasures, so that cheek to cheek male dancing offers the protectors of virtue an opportunity for intervention. This does not hinder homosexuals, who dance together when the cat's away, sometimes with ridiculous over-endearment. From time to time, a young inspector wearing a blazer and a cute face manages to find his way into one of these places, but the lovely cerberi who watch at the door usually have enough time to stop the music before an official report can be drawn up.

Anyway, they can feel perfectly free to dance the jerk in any discotheque with a partner as male as them, or do whatever they please in the homes of unusual-movie-and-pleasures fans.

★ Hotels: nothing could stop two men from demanding a conjugal bed while holding each other by the pinky, but they have to fill out a card. In Saint-Germain-des-Prés, an understanding hotel keeper will dispense with this formality, but has the tendency to raise the price. Everything can be bought. . . .

In Pigalle, hotelmanship is developed enough not to refuse any client. It can even be arranged to have a minet supplied with the room. Just ask for young Gérard or one of his cute friends on arrival.

Neo Women

Sometimes we can pick them out, but rarely can we figure them out; they haven't worked it out themselves. Transvestites, confused and exhibitionistic angels of darkness, are a step further than male homosexuality because they feel extremely "opposite," emphasized through hormones and surgery. But their civil status, taboos and neuroses condemn them to live on the edge of homosexuality. More feminine at heart and possibly in appearance than many women, these beings have acquired their femininity willfully, some with an unconscious obstinacy, others with lucid and desperate courage. In a world which has only recently accepted the pill, almost all of them pay dearly for having been crazy enough to become more than those "effeminate lunatics" by matching their hearts with their bodies.

These latter-day Eves who are self-created take refuge in the night because it is more tolerant and helpful than the day. But also because it is practically impossible for them to find a normal daytime female position, being born with male papers. It is easier to change anatomy than civil status. To the best of our knowledge, only Coccinelle (twice married) and one of her colleagues succeeded in legalizing in France their sexual metamorphosis. Too small a minority to present a real problem, despite the continuous flow of young men encumbered by their virility rallying to the cause. Complete transvestites can count only on bizarre British weddings or complicated and costly naturalizations in more tolerant countries.

A come-back to normal masculinity was already difficult in the days Dr. Von Krafft-Ebing studied in his enormous "Psychopathia sexualis" the men who felt like women. Turning back is unthinkable after years of hormone injections, impossible after the horrifying surgery of ablation and the semi-legal or clandestine plastic reshaping that takes place in Casablanca, Brussels, Baltimore or elsewhere. Transvestites who are not kept by their family or some protector can live only off the cabarets of prostitution. This explains the interest of the Mondaine, (more than the wear of feminine attire out of carnival season) in these inverts.

Many of the transvestites who solicit on the sidewalk, in cars, and in bars of the Champs Elysées or Pigalle wouldn't have behaved more properly had they retained their initial appearance. Feminine attire, long hair (or, in the case of some cheaters, wigs) make their work with curious and complacent, sometimes even astonishingly naive heteros, so much easier.

Transvestites who cog the dice and can hide their cumbersome secret—they are not all operated; far from it—still risk coming across a red-blooded male who, for his 100 francs, cares little about the things a near-woman does better or worse than a total-woman. Some of them succeed in working as call-girls, with an almost regular clientele (their generous admirers are usually heterosexual and sometimes very well-known . . . in other circles). Others fall to the depths of prostitution—under a procurer's watchful eye—and end up in the Bois de Vincennes at 20 francs per brief car ride.

The weaknesses of many venal transvestites inevitably lead them to the world of the "demi-sels" (small time punks) and shady homosexuals whom they cannot escape. A few rebel by squealing, but they quickly play back into the hands of the worst riff-raff. It also happens that honest and disinterested transvestites are condemned to prostitution, like the sad heroines of Zola. They fight for survival. . .

In various cabarets in and outside Paris, transvestite strippers are not introduced as such. At *Madame Arthur's* and *le Carrousel,* meeting grounds for transvestites from all over the world, they call them as they see them. Ninety per cent of the customers are stupefied by the extraordinary metamorphosis of the little sisters of Coccinelle. Their applause rings louder every time they are reminded of it. At *Madame Arthur's,* one can see the deep evolution which the little world of transvestism has been undergoing for the past 20 years: two races co-exist on stage.

Some of them are "artists," such as the amazing Maslowa, who comes in and leaves as a man. These performers are usually totally indifferent to heterosexuality. Nevertheless they don't intend to feminize themselves elsewhere than on the stage and find mutations induced by chemotherapy and surgery offensive. Their kind made the beautiful nights at the old *Carrousel,* on rue du Colisée. The floor shows were as good as the ones offered at *le Lido,* but the "girls" left the place in a vest-suits, after removing their make-up.

At times, a few real men appeared among the "mignons," with Pietral the dwarf, who was playing mini-Mae West. In short, they changed sexes for the sake of comedy or parody only.

Beside the inexhaustible Maslowa, Mme Sylva (who uses a very masculine name when appearing on television or at the theatre) and a few virile-looking ephebes, the hormoned queens plays it all the way. They leave in mink coats, real or imitation, and don't like to be reminded by "tantes-normal" (passive homosexuals) of their common origin. These women (permit us to use the feminine gender) feel at home at the *Carrousel,* a less amusing and less Rabelaisian cabaret than *Mme Arthur* but where the illusion is so strong that you never again will believe that civil status and a beard infalliably determine sex.

Transvestites who have committed themselves for life to hormones, a dress and sometimes the mini-skirt—some discotheques-minettes were minets once upon a time—can be recognized by their voice (a way to change vocal chords has not been discovered yet), the masculine narrowness of their hips and an unfeminine swelling at the throat and the triceps. Outsiders often say they knew it all along after somebody points it out to them, sometimes the interested party him(her)self.

The reactions of males who were deluded but who deny any interest in these males, range from a scornful, mocking or curious incomprehension to friendly and sometimes sensitive understanding. But the perpetual game of reality vs. illusion wears on the nerves of transvestites. Possibly because they are obsessed by a constant fear that they will give themselves away, some of them revert to provocative exhibitionism, reminiscent of the painful and self-destructive humor of certain minority groups.

Transvestites cheat nature so well that they sometimes become lesbians, but the uncertainties of the present, fear of the future and a certain physical frigidity makes the price very high.

Woman to Woman

Minettes who take life as it comes accept shamelessly the caresses and gifts of Lesbos. Idle and broke jerk-dancers readily lend their little bodies to robust ladies who judge women with a masculine eye. This is not real prostitution as it is found among male homosexuals. Not-so-moral little girls don't put a tag on their services, they are satisfied with modest considerations.

Most call-girls charge lesbians their usual prices, but a woman's lady friend likes neither cash payment nor a furtive embrace followed by a brutal separation. Many telephone prostitutes compensate by playing with their co-workers' bodies between jobs (free of charge); while retaining normal desires, call-girls and de-luxe prostitutes often feel perverse inclinations for their co-workers as well.

Apprentice lesbians who have their own interests in mind while permitting themselves to be initiated to sapphism, don't trade their hours of abandon. They usually take room and board and return cuddling. They accept pocket-money, dresses, and trips without feeling mercenary. In short they would rather be kept.

Lesbians don't play around as much as pederasts. In the night you could meet many nice female couples who take in a few slow dances (women dancing together is not prohibited by the Mondaine, but men dancing together is). There is nothing amusing about watching these women, who often take themselves very seriously.

With the exception of the young "garçonnes" who do their naive and somewhat outmoded number, lesbians spend their sleepless nights more discreetly than homosexuals. They will boldly dance close, but rarely around "normal" people, preferring to stay among their own kind. But don't delude yourself about the orthodoxy of clubs who play on the ambigueties of their feminine personnel. Among authentic lesbians you will find many venal cheaters. They play on the crusading feelings in men, who want to convert the misguided ladies, in addition, they are often willing to cheer up couples who have drained their repertoir of fun-for-two (estimate at least 300 F, for a long and intimate à trois).

Elle et Lui—one of the most successful Parisian cabarets—*le Monocle, Moune,* and the famous Frède's *Carroll's Club* star "garçonnes" but open their doors to a very healthy clientele that takes trips to the little world of Sappho of Lesbos. *Le Pousse-au-Crime* and the *Quodlibet* tolerate men well, but their habitués are clearly less sensitive to their virility than to the charms of the weaker sex. *Entre Nous* so very clearly shows the desire of its loyal clientele to stay among girls that you will meet there very few partisans of heterosexual persuasion. Less than at Frede's, though the latter's clientes too are convinced that it is better to stick to your own kind.

A few bars and restaurants could be added to this brief list of establishments where graceful and strange loves flourish, but the tour of the nocturnal world of lesbians is quickly over. The day may come when they will be starring once again as in the days when *le Carroll's* of rue de Ponthieu entered the legend of night . . .

CABARETS

(Strip-Tease/Typical Shows)

It so happens that vice, when poorly exploited or of bad quality, does not sell better than virtue. Most of the cabarets in Paris are not doing well and chances are they would not survive the reopening of cathouses and their parading ladies. Victimized by a bad reputation, sometimes exaggerated but on the whole well deserved, they often decline with neglect and become "gyp-joints." We don't sympathize with vulgar or intoxicated customers who get fleeced (except when they are foreigners), but we have come away with a very poor impression of these places.

Except for *le Lido* and *le Moulin Rouge*—the two large "nudie" factories—the amazing *Crazy Horse, the Sexy, Elle et Lui* and a few fair or bearable establishments, no part of Gay-Paris should figure in the most tolerant of night guide-books. The fatuous times of the *Florence* and the *Casanova,* the first *Carrousel* and *Carroll's* were gone by the time Porfirio Rubirosa left us for the play-boys' paradise.

The decadence of cabarets is due to several factors and not only to the indifference shown by General de Gaulle and his big financiers to the Common Market:

★ The fun frenzy that took hold of the French after the liberation could not last forever. Quickly satiated, men of the world and revellers abandoned night clubs in 1950.

★ After '55, discotheques monopolized the young who would have made up the clubs' new guard. Helped by the twist—that offered the side benefit of a free floorshow—discotheques gambled and won with relatively modest prices (changed since) and benefited from valuable publicity in the gossip columns too.

★ Some "michetons" ("johns") pay a check of 800 to 1000 francs in the hope, often in vain, to take a B-girl home when she goes off duty. Just as it happens that the profits of an easy young lady diminish considerably in a club where the client can have his own bottle, it is also simpler and more reliable to use the services of a call girl if you want more than a drinking companion. We have met some interestingly corrupt creatures in cabarets, and even ladies, whose only income there relates to the champagne consumed. But ten years' experience in night-life have taught us that it is better to take on the girls sung by Dutronc. . . . This does not mean you should rate the latter higher.

★ French prices have routed foreigners to friendlier countries. The misadventures of the pound sterling and the bad rapport between Johnson's America and the General's hexagone would have driven night-going Anglo-Saxons off for good had they not already rebelled against their exploitation. Americans, who are used to fixed prices and clear-cut tabs, refuse to understand our nocturnal scale of prices. On the whole, we agree with them, but they have a mean temper when they leave a cabaret unaccompanied.

★ The maître-d'hôtel's obsequious eagerness: his drive to keep the champagne flowing, the girls' unquenchable thirst, the sale of flowers, cigarets and perfume at exhorbitant prices, and the strictness of the 1-franc-restroom attendants leave a painful impression. Even if you like the atmosphere at a cabaret, even when 200 or 300 francs don't matter to you, it is hard to bear this harrassement. But then contact with lovely girls and fine alcohol does not sharpen our critical sense.

★ The clientele that is still attracted to cabarets is not always good company. Despite occasional forays by La Callas, the Buffets Curd Jurgens, Brel, the Onassises, Gunther Sachs or other club habitué's seeking a different scene, the vulgarity of noisy strip joint haunters cannot be overlooked. The flow of tourists pouring out of cars doesn't add refinement to these places, but these foreigners are too stunned to bother anyone. The head-waiter seats them in a corner where they stay put until the accompanist signals that the party is over. The quaintness of Pigalle still lives through a few cabarets that attract former inmates of Fresnes and la Santé. They too have a right to go to town between a stick-up and a conviction (they haunt familiar, genial places where they meet quietly at the bar.)

★ The spectacle . . . but is it a good show? Once in a while you can catch a superb girl under the spotlight of some shady joint, but we would have trouble extending the list of cabarets in this chapter without cheating. We may have sinned by omission, but we consider our list indulgent.

To the credit of cabarets—which we often find more "straightforward" than discotheques—we must note that certain owners still refuse to resort to kickbacks and watch taxis and girls turn clients away at their door, toward more generous places (it isn't easy to be driven directly to rue Brea or rue Vavin, where drivers don't receive compensations). Note also that the *Kit-Kat* and *la Dolce Vita* have a discotheque flavor and won't make club habitués feel lost. We also spent a full hour at the bar of *Eve,* smack in the center of Pigalle without once being pestered by a girl craving for a drink. . .

Very highly taxed by the "fisc" and carrying much higher expenses than discotheques, the cabaret is a den of thieves only to those who let themselves be robbed. Prices are posted and whiskey is often cheaper at the cabaret bar than in a club. We have pointed out the bad sides of this little world clearly enough to inform the client who wonders why bar-girls don't fall for his beautiful eyes!

In New York, Rome, Tokyo, or Rio, the company of girls is priced. When you know the game of these hostess-bars, you can choose to stay out of the place or out of the game. But you have to state your intentions clearly and make the girls understand that you won't be taken for a ride. The most eminent of our readers will be in the wrong if he decides to challenge the check after having called two girls over to his table and asked the orchestra to play songs from his youth...

Cabaret Girls

STRIPPERS

The Brigade Mondaine and morality forbid them to peel the last piece. Glued on with double-faced tape sold by the kilometer in Pigalle's pharmacies, a triangle baptised "pointe" permits the strip-teasers to hide that last mystery, their natural color. The rest, they divulge by taking off in 6 or 8 minutes a dress especially designed for piece by piece shedding. They would get rid of it much faster were it not for the fact that they are paid to make the suspense last.

It is extraordinary that strip-tease still exists in world where mini-skirts, Swedish films and Barbarella are common-place. The act of "looking" alone, sometimes followed up by priced carnal pleasures with partners who only rarely are the girls seen behind the ramp (it is not easy to undress the stripper who just finished dressing), however can still satiate the nocturnal sexual appetites of contemporary males.

A strange but touchy embarrassement floats about in strip-joints and it is not created by women who come to watch the uncovering of their shameless sisters. While the ladies in the audience often make a show of real or faked excitement, the more passionate observers often show a lack of courage when it comes to an expression of their approval. The clapping at the end of a strip-tease act is much weaker than the applause for a mediocre illusionist. Nobody asks for encores at the end of these compositions-without-words by virtuosos of progressive exposure.

Like any ordinary women but more attractive, which explains why not a single blush appears on their delicate skin when they peel, strip teasers obstinately insist on dressing just any old way when they are off duty. Too tired to take off their false eyelashes imprisoned behind dark glasses, and the body still tinted with a gilded bronze or walnut stain (natural pale complexions don't look good behind the footlights), they don't bother decorating their uncommonly desirable bodies. They look a fright when their hair is sloppily tucked in under a flappy Bonnie-bonnet, and their feet hidden by sewer-workers' boots. But before they meet their Clyde in some discotheque, they bring out their coquettishness. These night workers are too much admired on stage to seek approving looks in the street.

These honest women go home in a small bargain car or in a taxi they share with a friend who lives in the same direction. When they don't fall for the charms of their sisters-in-trade to the point of becoming lesbians (which occurs often enough) they often carry a family burden: a child rejected by his vanished father, a fiancé stricken with apathy, a grandmother to take care of, or a little brother to keep in school.

Strippers come mostly from a modest milieu and had to learn to survive at a very young age. Statistics show that they are rarely 100 per cent French: it seems that intermarriage and denudation are related. These dream creatures have as much Russian, Polish, German, Italian, or Arab blood as Breton, Landais or Provençal blood. They usually choose one of two kinds of living-quarters for their daytime rest:

★ A studio-kitchenette in an "immeuble-à-standing" on avenue Paul-Doumer, rue de Ponthieu or avenue de Neuilly is just right for a single and childless strip teaser. It is not a good idea to press for a friendly drink at her place. Many of these girls have the poor taste to share the apartment and the rent with a girl friend who does not desire to share the bed three ways.

★ H.L.M. (middle-income-housing) or better, situated outside of the Fermiers Généraux (former fortifications around Paris), are preferred by these charming creatures who all have families. When you take a stripper home beyond than the peripheral boulevards, you may as well give up hope for an immediate success. Even the most nymphomaniacal of girls could hardly frolic in a small apartment with convertible sofa and a large family. Your chances of success are inversly proportionate to the mileage covered after the portes d'Orléans, d'Ivy or de Vincennes . . . and to the reduction in the rent.

Since we seem to have arrived at the problem of corporal and egotistical use of strippers, let us specify that most of them are not mercenary. But if one decides to earn a mink, her prices would be prohibitive. If you strive to be loved for your delicate profile, your mind and your heart (in short, without loosening your wallet) you will have to:

★ Find the baby cute—if the lady has one—or have an understanding with a future mother-in-law who disapproves of her daughter's trade and would like her provided for;

★ Have the courtesy to consider strip-tease an art;

★ Delicately gather the false eyelashes scattered in the bathroom;

★ Ask the lady to take the make-up off her entire body before embracing you;

★ Bear valiantly the regular sessions of listening to rythmic music that might be right for a future act;

★ Leave in bed every morning a companion who will get up long after you have left for your laborious daily occupation.

If you are a gigolo, have your stripper offer you a copy of this guide, but don't expect her to add to it that little Porsche of your dreams. Strip-tease offers a better living than the teaching of Latin, but girls don't become millionaires by letting their bodies be carresses by eyes only. Certain big cabarets (very few) estimate that a couple of minutes of public immodesty are worth 80 or 90 F., but most girls are paid 20 to 25 francs per performance. This forces them to "double" in the same establishments or to disrobe in several joints . . . unless they cross the footlights and find themselves in the hall, dressed and thirsty for champagne.

Le Syndicat des Artistes de Variété does not allow owners to force the strippers to mingle with the clients, even when dressed. Bosses found a very simple gimick to get around this ruling. They put off engaging girls who refuse to keep the customers company till 4:30 or 5 a.m. Most of the girls, readily accept, and receive a cut of 15 or 20 francs per bottle-finished-off-with-a-client.

The hazards of nocturnal life don't prevent strippers from dreaming of new numbers created by homosexual or black choreographers (or both), with lighting similar to the *Crazy's*. Since the girls cannot count on the owners for advice, they choose their own music and tape it unless they can ask the piano-player in the joint to pick it up and adapt the score for orchestra—a more burdensome and less reliable solution, now abandoned.

These industrious ants have to prepare their own costumes before they can give anatomy lessons. They have their detachable dress cut and sewn by specialists of the ultra-gliding, never-jamming-zipper. And they shape their own "pointe." In a moment of madness they may buy a portable projector, or a black-light lamp on credit, hoping that a stage director will one day use it.

All this in order to show their body, as god created it, to more men in one evening than would most women in a life time. To close this chapter, displeasing some thirty cabaret owners, we suggest you improve your knowledge of anatomy at the *Crazy*, the *Sexy, Elle et Lui,* the *Kit-Kat* and *la Dolce Vita*. While remembering the partucularly interesting cases you, could meet at the *Folies-Pigalles, Chez Eve* at the *Pussy Cat, la Villa, la Parisienne* and *Lucky* . . . maybe somewhere else too, but only accidentally.

BAR GIRLS

Their salaries are not impressive. A hostess does not earn more than 600 F. a month without her cuts of 10 to 15 francs per turned over bottle of champagne. In the darkness, these "fiancées" have have a heart to heart (and sometimes body to body) talk with their customers because they must drink and make others drink for a living. After 6 hours of waiting at the bar, of verbal tenderness, cuddling and champagne, they are free to use their body as they wish. After their envelopes are distributed at dawn (they are paid daily) they can negotiate their anatomy if they want to, if there is a taker.

Some do it—in a joint with hostesses it can be negotiated—others prefer to go back to their true loves. The chasseur, barman, or the maître d'hôtel (head waiter) won't be annoyed if you ask them the question discreetly. They will point out which lady you can count on to end a mad champagne-night in joyful and priced lovemaking (prices vary with current rates, similar to the ones paid to call girls). At four or five o'clock in the morning the management has no interest to watch the behavior or misbehavior of its girls.

It might be simpler to reopen the "maisons," but c'est la vie, c'est la nuit!—and it is the same all over the world. Since a cabaret with B-girls is officially a show-establishment with a "license IV" (for alcohol sale) and not a brothel, the brigade mondaine (vice squad) does not allow the girls to leave before the paycheck. There is no way of leaving with a client and returning an hour later.

Forbidden fruit has its charms, so they do sneak out at times, but rarely. Even if the police have to turn away from the petty and ridiculous abuses of night life, the tavern-keepers don't gain much by defying the law, or by letting customers leave when they could still consume a few bottles waiting for closing time.

The hostesses can be pretty, but the frankly ugly ones and the old-hawks can get into the action too . . . because they go all the way and because psychology counts for much in this profession, just as in salesmanship. The fat darlings who feed their obesity on alcohol in cabarets, want attention

One lucid girl tells us, "It is essential to hook them and get them to uncork the first bottle. Once they have started drinking, they let go more easily.

"Most of these characters are not maniacs, even if they are licentious. They are people who have worked hard all their life, earned a lot of money and are now bored. They want to chat, to have some diversion. They are sick of their wives, of their daily worries. They need to be fussed over, to be told what they no longer hear at home: 'You are handsome, you're smart, you're nice.'

"Men are not used to compliments. If you know how to give them, they are more flattered than the most coquettish woman.

"You also have to let them talk. One often feels that they want to confess. They tell you their life story, bragging, complaining, evoking wife and kids. They can go as far as to show you their picture. If the girl knows how to go about it, even if she ends up leaving them at 4 a.m., she will leave them with no regrets when faced with the check. Some might even leave a tip. Many come back."

A customer has the right to have a drink at the bar all alone, without having to offer one to a thirsty girl. The cleverest and prettiest B-girls always manage to be taken care of. When a customer does not have the good manners to be easily hooked, the barmaid plays cupid for a percentage and remarks that "mademoiselle is very thirsty" (keep in mind that the barmaid is thirsty too). If this does not work, a girl will feel a mad urge to dance with a handsome though scornful loner. After a few slows, the reticent customer will discover that dancing makes him thirsty.

At dawn, a good number of girls are lightly tipsy, despite their schooling in hostessing. But they know how to keep from getting drunk. When there are no customers, they accept a few rare drinks offered by the management and sit around bored, or chatter on. Even when there isn't a soul in the place, they can't leave before the ordained hour-of-the-envelope.

But these poor creatures must be even more bored in the company of some customers. Listening to the conversation of verbose and noisy tavern-haunters, one begins to understand why lesbians are such good hostesses. It is easy for girls who do not appreciate the charms of the stronger sex to scorn them smilingly . . . for money.

Strip-Tease Joints

Le Crazy Horse Saloon. 12, avenue George-V, 225-69-69.

Recently doubled in size when they acquired their own door on the street (for 26 years you had to enter through the yard). People still pile in lightheartedly to the point of confusing their own table with their neighbor's. The waiters who manage to glide through like ectoplasms between German hips and Yankee shoulders, are the only ones capable or orienting themselves in this human magma mesmerized by Alain Bernardin's strippers.

Bernardin is not only the owner of the *Crazy* (opened in 1951 in a coal bin nobody wanted), he is the *Crazy*. His taste, including an inkling for provocation, his moods, his neurotic excesses, his extreme sense of the nonsensical, his whims are reflected in each number as well as in the decor or the variety of folders clients find on their table before the show.

He obstinately serves impossible cocktails—no other cabaret-keeper dare sell—to the mass of dunces impressed by the international fame of the house and to the sophisticated clientele that converts the *Saloon* or the tiny manager's office into their drawing room. Texan oil-tycoons and designers in the Courrège style, Belgian tourists and secondhand "Play-Boy" readers all are ready to discover Bernardin's version of "woman." Salvador Dali, Paco Rabanne, Alain Robbe-Grillet, Henri-Geroges Clouzot or Lucchino Visconti feel as much at ease at the *Crazy* as Frank Sinatra, Gina Lollobrigida, exhibitors at the Salon de Cuir or provincial visitors to the Salon de l'Auto.

That the owner of *Crazy* does everything his own way and still satisfies the most varied of clienteles is a paradox.

Remarkable visual acts alternate with denudations staged by Bernardin, but the *Crazy Horse* is most of all a laboratory where the strip-tease of tomorrow is contrived. In this avant-garde cabaret the girls don't just peel, but perform 8-minute musical comedy numbers in which the stars unveil their irreproachable anatomies magnified by lighting.

The *Saloon* has weaknesses too, when for instance Bernardin does not "feel" the new number or when he holds on too long to an undressing act and it becomes mechanical with time.

Yet it still is the only Parisian cabaret where you can discover something new. The new sound, magic lantern projections, frenzied flashes, parodies and humor to make your teeth grate (as when they combine Hitler and the swastika with the exhibitions of a sculptural German girl with grand proportions). These innovations can almost take your mind off the beautiful bodies carefully selected by a fanatic of female anatomy.

At the *Crazy*, a woman is not simply unveiled but rather revealed in style. Sexual obsessions are ever present but kept at a distance: amateurs of coarse jests and French jokes might be as disappointed as the attentive men watching for well rounded breasts or a plump rump.

Over 15 years after he came close to bankrupcy with *Rose Rouge* type shows (clothed) that featured Fernand Raynaud, Charles Aznavour, Georges Wilson and François Patrice, Bernardin sells for 52 francs (2 drinks payable in advance, plus service 15%) his personal interpretations of the female body, between 11 p.m. and 2 a.m. Nobody leaves during the intermission (with the King Fanfan orchestra), so you would be wise to make a reservation if you wish to add new names to your personal list of "crazyrotic" contemporaries which may include Rita Renoir, Yoko Tani, Rita Cadillac, Cha Londres and Dodo of Hambourg, the first in Paris to unzip more cleverly than in the bedroom.

Le Crescendo. 40, rue du Colisée, 225-11-68.
Took over the quarters of the old *Carrousel* . . . without keeping its stars.

The owners of this vast and luxurious place that caters mostly to a foreign and provicial clientele recently gave up supper shows. A few good visual numbers, occasionally daring strip acts and discreet "hôtessens." Refreshments are 20 francs at the bar and 35 at the table, plus service. A bottle of champagne goes for 120 F.

Eve. 7, place Pigalle, 878-37-96.
Belongs to the brothers Pierini and their brother-in-law. These discreet Corsicans reign at *la Nouvelle Eve* (reopened in May of 1968) and *l'Eden* too. This cabaret, hardly original, offers three shows at 10 p.m., 11:15 p.m., and 1:15 a.m. to a clientele that is mostly foreign and that often arrives by car.

The two local B-girls have enough manners not to attack the clients with the disgusting fervor of their neighborhood sisters. You can have a drink at the bar (25 francs a scotch) without suffering venal assaults, or peacefully sit at a table with a friend (40 francs the shot). Introduced by Louis Massis—who has style, but is at times too talkative—the show keeps a good pace.

We were completely overwhelmed by the daughters of Eve, who offer fresh nudity on stage. In Pigalle, where the queens of the bars often have flabby breasts and fortyish buttocks, it is pleasant to find naked little jerkers you can invite to *Régine* or *Castel's* after reluctantly asking them to put their clothes back on.

Le Fifty-Fifty. 26, rue Fontaine, 874-27-93.
Does not switch its neon lights off until the late hours of dawn. When cleaning trucks spray away from rue Fontaine the last vestiges of the night, a mixed clientele—local, provincial, and sometimes foreign—empty the last bottles of champagne with hostesses who sleep during the day. Unpretentious shows, usually very uncovered, sometimes bawdily funny.

Refreshments are 16:50 F. (minimum) at the bar and champagne is 112 per bottle, not including service.

Les Folies-Pigalle. place Pigalle, 878-25-56.
Belongs to Mme Martini but is managed by her sister Alice. It is hard to miss the cascade of lights and the diamond shapes that form the ·facade of this cabaret that looks more like a theatre (the room was recently raised so the distance of the audience from the stage would not be too Brechtian).

Vince Taylor, the "blouson noir" archangel of the budding twist, had starred—like Nancy Holloway—in a variety show. The première was applauded by Tout-Paris (in tuxedos) who had long forgotten Pigalle. Later the formula was abandoned, but you can still see at the *Folies* good visual acts and splendid creatures whose charms take gloriously to footlights, since this cabaret has real ramp-lights.

Minimum rate for a drink at the bar: 12.50 F. without service. Champagne is 80 F. in the room, plus the percentage.

Le Jockey. 127, boulevard du Montparnasse, 326-48-93.
Hides its loose and outdated fun behind an unusual streaked facade, across the boulevard from *Régine*. No connection with the *New Jimmy's* or the *Jocky Club!* This cabaret is of another era. Its clientele, over forty years of age, indulges in noisy laughter and chatter. It is enlivened by a Miss Jockey whose function consists of exclaiming regularly, "Ca, c'est jockey" ("This is jockey")—and anything can fill the bill.

Le Kit-Kat Saloon. 23, rue Bréa, 326-95-73.
Jean Fradel made a night owl's stop at this cabaret between

l'Elephant Blanc and *le Tekki,* but Roger Renou, the place's discreet soul is still there. Old timer in night life, he watches over his place like a professional without making himself obvious.

We cannot give you an exact schedule of entertainment but we guarantee superb anatomies on stage—and delightful barmaids behind the bars. Prices (under 21 francs) like the acts are honest. A clientele of habitués; hostesses—often pretty—who know better than to stick to indifferent loners.

Le Lucky-Strip. 4, rue Arséne-Houssaye, 225-56-66.

The debonnaire M. Emil, who took over the place after the failure of *le Caramel,* and his athletic assistant don't seem to place much importance upon the metaphysics of strip-tease. They do know how to recruit strippers and hostesses whose plastic qualities we found appealing.

On first contact, a scotch (18 francs) at the quaint pub-bar or at the table (30 francs) may suffice. If on the other hand, you wish to remake the world in the company of a "demoiselle de la maison", order champagne to quiet her unquenchable thirst (120 francs the bottle).

La Parisienne. 36, rue de Ponthieu, 359-46-60.

Succeeded the *Saint-Hilaire* and the *Carroll's* in quarters that have known glorious nights and sinister interludes. This place, newly transformed into a cabaret, has a pleiad of pretty girls to undress on stage and to be courted in the hall. A few good acts, such as Mir and Mirovska. Drinks are 21 francs (bar) and 30 F. (table). Story lovers will pop the corks more cheerfully when they find out that *la Parisienne* is set up on the very spot the old rendez-vous house of the countess de Ponthieu was located...

Le Pussy-Cat. 22, rue Quentin-Bauchart, 225-08-51.

Presents good entertainment and a rather funny M.C.—when in shape—to excite Alain Bernardin when he takes off from his *Crazy Horse.* No less evident is the fact that the customers of the *Pussy-Cat* love the numerous and "fascinating kittens of Paris" who crawl all over the place. They know how to purr in front of a glass of champagne (140 to 160 the bottle, service included), but at times will accept a scotch (30 francs). It is hard to ignore them. They are very attractive.

Le Sexy. 68, rue Pierre-Charon, 225-25-17 and 18.

Is managed by M. and Mme Perrault. In 1958, the Perraults opened this place instead of a chinese restaurant, with two beginners called Marten and Devos. As the clientele of the Champs-

Elysées grew more and more international, they moved toward the visual. Now the program consists of seven strip-tease acts, and seven no-talk numbers. The *Sexy* is one of the best Parisian cabarets.

A few B-girls, pretty and polite, accept a drink with clients at the bar, but they are not allowed to put their charm to work at the tables, where many couples are seated. After the show the orchestra moves to a small room where you can stay up with a last drink.

The program, created by Mme Perrault, begins at 11:30 and ends at 2:30 (five minute breaks between numbers. There is usually no intermsision). The strippers can be proud of their bodies, the decor is classical and clean—a rare phenomenon in cabarets. Drinks are 40 francs at tables, service included; refills at 23 francs. A shot at the bar is 23 francs.

La Villa. 27, rue Bréa, 326-64-85.

Puts on 4 shows between 11 p.m. and dawn. Most of the pretty girls who undress on the stage mingle later with the clients. They will appreciate your conversation if you can appreciate champagne (120 F. per bottle) that Mr. Farry, the boss, chose discriminately. He happens to be in the champagne business himself, exporting this noble drink to America. Instead of recording with Barclay or Pathé, the doorman sometimes, appears on stage and proves to all that he did not lose his voice hailing taxis for clients. *La Villa* makes full house during the big salons. The clientele seems to have fun there, if we can judge by the paper streamers that pile up on the sidewalk outside.

Refreshments are 20 francs, the bottle of champagne 130 francs, service included.

"*Specialized*" Cabarets

le Carrousel. 29, rue Vavin, 326-66-33.

A thin partition separates the ladies of next-door *Elle et Lui*, who would rather be gentlemen, and the young men-become women thanks to hormones and possibly plastic surgery. Transvestites performing at *le Carrousel* don't share the stage with real-women during their feathered nudie show. The most intransigeant heterosexuals could forget the civil status of the ambiguous stars of acquired femininity. A slight hoarseness may eventually give away the official identity of these strippers who go as far as that little "pasty"—the minimum required by the Mondaine (vice squad). At neighboring *Mme Arthur's* one can still feel nostalgic for the true-transvestites who just disguised themselves. At *le Carrousel* the metamorphosis is total. A legend about rue Vavin tells of a performer at No. 29 who found his virility to marry a re-converted "garçonne" (aggressive lesbian) from No. 31, but this paradoxical anecdote will probably remain a unique case, all regrets being superfluous after a fateful trip to Casablanca.

Transvestites from all over the world besiege M. Marcel, who had launched the first *Carrousel* on rue du Colisée in the days when a transvestite had to resort to painful injections to grow a bust. Also the organizer of shows on tour and owner of *Mme Arthur,* he launched Coccinelle, Bambi, Fétiche and other stars of successful eonism.

Elle et Lui. 31, rue Vavin, 633-29-59.
It is "elle" (she) seeing herself as "lui" (he). But the "garçonnes" of this constantly busy cabaret don't dissuade gentlemen from watching the strip shows, sometimes daring, graced by beautiful creatures. La Callas, Juliette Gréco, Françoise Sagan, Curd Jurgens and Salvador Dali have sat around the dance-floor-stage: there isn't enough distance from the stage at *Elle et Lui,* but nobody minds it.

Four shows run consecutively till dawn, their stars fascinate the "garçonnes," dressed in chieftain-style, as much as the male clientele that packs the bars (at Montparnasse, they like barmaids and multiple bars). Maria Vincent, a talented performer who did not exploit her talents fully had played Marilyn of the French song at this cabaret. The entertainment is good but you will remember the impudent duos and superb unveiled anatomies most of all.

Elle et Lui, both a cosmopolitan and very Parisian cabaret, has a fair price rating. You may borrow a pretty hostess from the garçonnes and have a mad champagne party together, but the price list is honestly posted: 19 francs (service included) at the bar and 29 F. at a table (100 francs for a bottle of champagne). The personnel is mannerly enough not to push drinking.

Madame Arthur. 75 bis, rue les Martyrs, 076-48-27.
Has a rather normal clientele. After a moment of stupor, the women-women applaud as hard as their husbands the extraordinary metamorphosis of the transvestites introduced by Maslowa, a former classical ballet dancer now "animatrice" (female master of ceremonies) in the only cabaret on Pigalle where people crowd every night all year long.

We think the world of *Madame Arthur* and so we would like to get the criticism over with: the sound system is frankly mediocre, the spiciness of a few sketches comes close to vulgarity, the singers in long dresses don't all sound like Nana Mouskouri. But this matters very little with these ravishing illusions who don't even hint at their civil status.

Maslowa is a gracious gentleman of 56 who, every night after applying make-up for an hour, changes into a mistress of ceremonies. Indefatigably "she" harasses the audience, forcing laughter out of them and leading the show at an infernal tempo. Maslowa, who for a long time had danced very classically—and not in a tutu—has been playing the role of Madame Arthur these last 20 years. She identifies with the cabaret she manages from 11 p.m. to 4 a.m. without worrying about the sacrosanct daily rest.

Cuddled in a boa, at times wearing a mini-dress, with a hat à la Garbo, Maslowa shouts shocking things, carries the pun beyond the absurd, goes overboard . . . and has a hold on her public like few other entertainers. Next to her, the transvestites with hormones who unveil charms as unmasculine as possible, seem like very proper young ladies.

The stars of the show belong officially to the male sex (only Coccinelle—formerly of this joint—was able to obtain a change in her civil status). Two kinds of transvestites work side by side on the narrow stage of *Mme Arthur*. The artists who make it a point of honor to come and leave as men, and the "hormoned" ones who would be very miserable if they were forced to wear a men's suit. To spend an evening with these sometimes very beautiful creatures of another world will cost you 28 F. (price of a drink at the table, service included). . . . And if you find out that Fernand Raynaud made his debut at *Madame Arthur's,* don't jump to conclusions. He put on a very "normal" comedy sketch.

Other Very Specialized Cabarets
—chez Frida. corner rue Pigalle and rue Victor-Macé, 744-93-75.
—le Monocle. 60, bd Edgar-Quinet, 326-41-30.
—la Montagne. 46, rue de la Montagne-Ste-Geneviève.
—chez Moune. 54, rue Pigalle, 744-64-64.

Shows and Reviews

Le Lido. 78, Champs-Elysées, 359-11-61.
Is now 40 years old. This cabaret, as well known to foreigners as the Eiffel tower, was taken over by the Clerico brothers after the liberation. It was originally opened in 1929 by Léon Volterra, who bought this immense place including a fantastic dance-pool where gondolas glided on Venetian festival nights.

The Coliseum orchestra's fox-trots are long since forgotten and all that is left of the pool is a big empty space under the stage. Joseph and Louis Clerico, entrepreneurs who turned to variety shows (they like them somptuous, colorful and uncovered), have entrusted Paris' largest cabaret to Pierre-Louis Guérin. Since "Confetti," his first hit show, this director-stage-manager has created variety shows every two years that are borrowed by Las Vegas. Shows with American pagentry and foreign stars but French flavor.

Le Lido is light, cascades of water and fire, costumes that make you dream of Carnaval in Rio, a giant ice-skating ring, big international acts and the orchestra of Ben, a moustachioed specialist of the cha-cha who proved his talent in Havana at the invitation of the Cuban government. But *le Lido* is also the permanent ballet of the Blue Bell Girls, whose sculptural beauty is matched by the vast stage. Miss Blue Bell, the benevolent but absolute boss of these tall girls, whose height varies from 1.75 to 1.85 meters (barefoot!), is herself only 1.66 m, but keeps her girls in line with Irish authority. In fact, she is Irish and her name is Kelly. Her parents gave her the nickname Blue-Bell when she was studying classical ballet.

Stars of the entire spectacle at *le Lido* which they animate from end to end with their feathered and thrilling semi-nudity, the Blue Bell Girls obediently appear at 10:15 and leave at 3. They are strictly forbidden to meet the public anywhere but from the other side of the footlights. Even their parents cannot join them backstage. The little stairway leading to their dressing room is more strictly guarded than the entrance to an atomic plant.

16 to 26 years old, these Blue Bell Girls are British, German, Swiss, Dutch and even French. Most of them live in studios right above *le Lido* during their three or four year stay, some-

times longer. After their training in Paris two thirds of the 80 adopted daughters of Miss Blue Bell work abroad in ballets she controls via telecommunications (a show in Las Vegas every 16 months).

When Blue Bells leave the company it is often for matrimonial reasons. Unfortunately it is hard to court them, even if you feel "up" to it. Unapproachable at *le Lido,* the girls go out in groups when they feel like dancing after work and don't make it easy for discotheque bachelors to approach them.

You may have to be satisfied with just looking at them. Half a bottle of champagne is 50 francs at *le Lido* (service included) dinner is usually 78 f, but you can pick fixed-price dinners for 83, 92 and 97 francs . . . or à la carte. The bar is far from the stage, but prices are inversely aproportionate to the distance: 25 F the drink.

Le Moulin Rouge. place Blanche, 606-78-02 and 606-00-19.

Is as old as the Eiffel Tower and Maurice Chevalier. Launched one again in 1961, the ball has existed since 1889, since the French can-can of the "Quadrille naturiste", Toulouse Lautrec and Yvette Guilbert. Léon Volterra sold programs there before creating *le Lido* . . . which he later surrendered to the Clericos, the present owners of the revived Moulin-Rouge. Robert Rouzaud, overseer in charge of the big machinery of the variety show in F ("Frou-frou," "Flutter," "Fascination"), directs 70 artists, 22 musicians, 15 wardrobe girls, 15 machinists, and 50 waiters and barmen. Every night his heart stops beating when the elevator lifts the 16 ton pool where the girl-sirens, grand daughters of La Goulue, evolve gracefully. La place Blanche is built over an old plaster quarry—explaining its name —so that concrete was injected up to 16 meters in depth to fortify the foundations of this giant aquarium.

They come in taxis, cars and sometimes Rolls Royces to see the Doriss Girls led by Miss Doris, a good dancer from Germany. She arrived from Stuttgart on a bicycle to dance at *le Tabarin.* Now she teaches her girls how to look naked or adorned but never crude. The numbers are international and so is the clientele (same as at *le Lido*: they are not even aware of being in Pigalle). During the Salon de l'Auto, 80 per cent of the 1000 spectators are French, but the ratio is inverted in July.

The dinner-dancing starts at 9 p.m. and the show at 11:00. A second performance is given at 1 in the morning. You can have a drink at the bar for 20 francs, but most customers prefer a half-bottle of champagne for 50 francs at the table. The waiters are well mannered and attentive, despite the spaciousness of the place.

Other shows. in the following "theatres":
—Casino de Paris. 16, rue de Clichy, 874-26-22.
—Concert Mayol. 10 rue de l'Echiquier, 770-95-08.
—Folies-Bergères. 32, rue Richer, 770-98-49.

Exotic Cabarets

Frenchmen care little about bellydances, oud music or monotonous Oriental sounds. The Spaniards and Russians alone have succeeded in penetrating the Parisian night. They are part of the family with their well-known élan, their ardour and melancholy.

The Spaniards, victims of the exchange rate of the peseta and the crumbling luxury buildings by the water near Valencia, struggle to hold their heads up. Their flamenco in Paris is often more genuine than the one offered to tourists in Madrid and Barcelona, yet the French tourists who have seen and heard it at unbeatable prices in its original setting are suspicious. Family or group trips to a Spain which is both enriched and stifled by a heavy flow of tourism, has given them a taste for authenticity—the very taste that drives them to buy brand new Louis XVs and charming little farms in Eure-et-Loir.

Despite the "why hear again in Paris what was better in Madrid" attitude of Frenchmen, a few flamenco and zapateado night-spots still maintain a loyal clientele, though not necessarily a well-to-do or all-night. Among them are many students whose diligent attendance at the Sorbonne often brings out a taste for Spanish guitar besides a liking for jazz and strong opinions on Vietnam. This gives a few legitimate cabarets the opportunity to feature Spanish musicians who would rather perform for the tourists in his homeland.

Russians buy dead souls, make revolutions, down their vodka in a single motion then break the glass, and with their shoes they have been known to bang on tables at the UN. These are the mad Russians. They wept when Stalin died as they lamented the passing of the tzar and bygone Russia. They speak of suicide when hearing "Dark Sunday," and when they listen to a passionate singer tell the heartbreaking story of the boublichkis vendor they commiserate by stuffing themselves with boublichkis. These are the melancholy Russians.

First to admit that they are mad and melancholy—in other words truly Russian—the Slavs who arrived at the same time as Chagall and Diaghilev will stoop to paying gypsies and seek in champagne memories of the boundless Ukraine and majestic Don . . . if they did not resolve before the war to buy a cabaret rather than be its doorman. Gifted in languages, their sons have polished their accents, temperaments, and balalaikas to entertain Paris with Russian grandeur. Today, Russian nights are violent, sanely licencious, luxuriously fascinating and costly.

In 1923, after a scramble with the Corsicans in Montmartre, these robust and rough white Russians hung their sabres up on the walls of *le Caveau Caucasien* (fortunately for M. Paoli, and his *Etoile de Moscou,* peace has long since been declared). Heavy drinkers and excellent dancers, solid Caucasians opened Parisian night life to princes who had abandoned their geneological trees in Soviet Russia and were feeding their insomnia on the champagne served at *Kasbek,* an overcrowded little cabaret where drinks flow till the cars parked outside.

Monseigneur and *Sheherazade* were launched in 1928, *Don Juan* in 1935. The years of the charleston (and ballet russes!) were shared with cossack dances, gypsy fugues and deep melancholy. The tragic fire at *Casanova* (two dead on Russian new year 1938, because the doors opened toward the inside), then the war, were not about to prevent well-off Parisians from leading the life of grand-dukes. Violins did not stop crying till after the Liberation. The fifties were unfavorable for cabarets. For a full decade, night-time Russians had their *Berezina* and then a long recession, despite a final craze for the prolonged dinners at *Dinarzade. Casanova* was built for a brilliant and ephemeral career but Russian nights are as eternal as the mother country. While Tout-Paris went jerk-happy in new anglicized discotheques, the emigrants, their sons and newcomers from the East revitalized the party (Régine who is partly Slav pitched in too, with the *Reginskaia* in Deauville and occasional mad gypsy nights at *New Jimmy's*). While Russians in the U.S.S.R.

were ascending still higher in the spatial night, the Slavs at Clichy and l'Etoile were penetrating deeper in the hearts of Parisians.

The octogenarian cimbalom players are as spirited today as in their twenties and the musicians in Marc de Loutchek's orchestra average twenty years of age. The extraordinary Valia Dimitrievitch is still there with a girl whose proud and sumptuous beauty miraculously escaped the sharp-eyed talent scouts. Moscow's and Saint Petersberg's legendary nights shine as bright in 1968 as in their youth.

Ethnic-establishment hunters are advised to carefully examine other chapters in this ultra-guide. In the chapter on discotheques, for instance, they will find places like *la Plantation* that will satisfy their hunger for the picturesque. Among the restaurants they might like to look into *le Baobab, la Montagne Pelée, le Requin Chagrin* and a few others.

SPANISH CABARETS

La Candelaria. 3, rue Monsieur-le-Prince.
Offers flamenco, South-American folkstyles, guitar and Indian harp. There is no bar in the place but you can stand near the cash register with a glass of whiskey or settle down with a jug of "sangria" (Madeira with water, sugar and grated nutmeg). The clientele consists in the main of students who crave the "paella-maison" (Spanish dish with rice base) but who keep their forks still when Rafael de Granada or the Calchakis perform. In this elongated hall, a show-dinner costs no more than 30 francs, whiskey 15 francs, and sangria 8 francs. The show is interesting and varigated. You may have trouble finding a seat.

A small avant-garde "café-théâtre" on the lower level.

El Catalan 16, rue des Grancs-Augustins, 326-46-07.
Its dancers, singers and guitarists entertain from two platforms: one is located at the bar (about 10 F per drink, 20 at the table), the other on the first floor where you can sup on paella and flamenco for 40 or 45 francs. The days when Picasso would interpret a guitar arabesque on the tablecloth—in front of Eluard and Cocteau—are gone now, but real lovers of

Spanish atmosphere still dwell at el Catalan, among a few studious tourists. First coplas (Catalan musical group) at about 9:30 p.m. (closed on Sunday)

Don Quijote. 10, rue Rochambeau, 878-01-80.
Opens late enough to welcome guitarists and singers (from other cabarets) playing here for their own enjoyment after the official flamenco has been put to sleep with most tourists. Tables are rare but the place serves a hearty paella and plain but sincere Spanish specialties. Instead of dining you can keep time to the music and consume trans-Pyrennean wines (for 30 F).

La Guitare. 14, rue Hautefeuille, 326-41-11.
Offers from 10:30 on an enthusiastic little group, a "cuadro," that did not loose its sparkle in Paris. After seeing the dancing girls, you are bound to return to this place! Refreshments are 15 francs. (Closed on Sunday)

La Venta. 33, rue Guénégard, 326-69-83.
Offers its spicy dinners (service till at least one in the morning) its guitars, dancers and Basque setting for some 45 francs. Waiters wearing noiseless canvas shoes move as fast as "pelotari" and gladly teach clients the proper way to use the "poron" —to prevent wine-stained ties.

The dancers are consumed with a flamenco flame. The room, with its beautiful stone walls is spacious but cosy, and the kitchen—where you can smell the wonderful fragrance of olive oil—is honestly Iberian. A drink is 10 francs at the bar and 20 at the table. (Closed on Sunday)

RUSSIAN CABARETS

L'Etoile de Moscou. 6, rue Arsène-Houssaye, 359-63-12.
Rose in the nocturnal sky of the Champs Elysées thanks to Jacques Paoli, a Corsican who also reigns over *la Villa d'Este* and *la Caravelle,* all three on the same street. When he decided to open in quarters formerly occupied by Jean Méjean's *le Zèbre à Carreaux,* and *le Paris Dinner's,* he called upon M. and Mme Novsky, who had given their name to the *Novy* (still in existence, just a few steps from avenue Paul-Doumer). Nadia and Victor Novsky arrived with their retinue. Their longtime experience in slavic night life taught them how to keep the languor and frenzy of gypsy violins and Russian balalaikas going.

At least 60 to 70 francs per dinner, but vodka and champagne will lead you further astray. 30 F the drink.

Karpoucha. 12, rue Paquier, 265-53-10.
Was opened by Ter Abramov, the greatest balalaika player this side of the Iron Curtain. This very, very old gentleman and the triangular instrument he plays like a virtuoso have attracted all the children and grandchildren of slavic emigrants to the elegant little room on rue Pasquier.

You dine at *Karpoucha* for about 60 francs and don't be embarrassed to invite real Russians there. They know the place already. (Closed on Sunday)

Kortchma. 4, villa Guelma, 076-18-52.
Has set up business not far from Place Pigalle but has no ties with its surroundings. It is certainly the least expensive place where you can have boublichkis while listening to the song they inspired.

Kortchma, a charming old-fashioned Russian inn rather than a restaurant featuring show-suppers, offers a home made "borscht," good "chachliks" and plain unassuming musicians who are quite talented yet don't expect you to hand them a 10 francs bill (gypsy musicians usually do). The atmosphere—intimate, pleasant—and the check of only 55 francs for two will encourage you to come in again.

Monseigneur. 94, rue d'Amsterdam, 874-25-35.
Was sent off long before the war, by Sacha and Leonide Bronstein, Mosjoukin's good friends and princes in Russian night life. Parisians who had fallen in step with the slavik trend *chez Kasbek* and at *le Caveau Caucasien,* remained loyal to *Monseigneur's* violins till after the liberation, despite competition from *Casanova, Don Juan* and *Sheherazade...*

The cabaret reopened after a three year closing and despite its prestigious name and revived violins, it did not hit it off.

Roughly 200 francs for a supper-for-two: if your companion likes velvet, lustre and bubbling strings that can sing caressingly too, you won't regret it. Of course you could very easily spend much more.

Novy. 6, rue Faustin-Hélie, 870-02-33.
Is more a restaurant-with-show than a cabaret. The blond Douka, and the lovely singers in Marc de Loutchek's young orchestra may come over to the tables once in a while, but stay only the time of a refrain. These girls are fresh and spontaneous and they know how to step aside for a veteran of the

grand Russian nights who hams up his number masterfully. The unbelievable Valodia Poliakoff, over eighty years old and brother of Serge Poliakoff, is full of animation when Onassis or La Callas makes an appearance. Every night, Valia, Thereza and Aliocha Dimitrievitch exhibit their gypsy talent. They are sometimes accompanied by the go-go youngsters of the balalaika: Marc de Loutchek's musicians.

If they happen to be playing at the Novy—which needs redecorating—we suggest you spend a short but sweet Russian evening there.

Eliminate 50 to 90 F per person, for supper. Scotch is 25 F and a bottle of champagne is 100 to 120 francs.

Raspoutine. 58, rue de Bassano, 359-04-31.
Brigitte Bardot felt slavic there, especially since she came in the company of Günther Sachs. The royal family of Morocco, Gina Lollobrigida and Robert Hossein—of Russian origin—had a vodka supper with balalaika music.

Raspoutine is Mme Martini's second Russian cabaret-restaurant. She also owns Shéhérazade. Located in supposedly cursed rooms, this joint had a fast start under the strong management of a Russian with a very French name—André (he trained at *Casanova*).

Raspoutine does not owe its success to the neutral slavic food served there as much as to its haunting red setting, its cushioned benches and its thirty musicians, singers and dancers. They arouse a wonderful enthusiasm in the clients. It may not be spontaneous but it is very catchy.

Gypsy violins and Russian balalaikas stop only to let Alois Bologh, an extraordinary old gentleman of 83, who handles the cimbalom masterfully, exhibit his talents. He alone would justify a stop at *Raspoutine's*. Have a whiskey or vodka at the bar (16.50 and 14 F plus 20% for service) and listen to this unusual virtuoso of the "Hungarian vibraphone".

If you want to spend a long evening there, we advise you to wait for a moneyed first of the month. To fully enjoy the place you must immerse yourself in the mood and play the game fully (preferably in the company of a girl who can take her vodka and champagne). The check will go as high as 120 or 150 francs for supper, but you will get an uninterrupted show till 3 or 4 a.m. and maybe a chance to roll under the table like a cossack....

Shéhérazade. 3, rue de Liège, 874-41-68.
Was reopened in 1928, when immigrants brought the lost

motherland to Paris. Michel, the manager, has been with the place for 20 years, but this thousand-and-one-nights cabaret in a crypt-like setting belongs to Mme Marini who also owns *les Folies-Pigalle* and *le Fifty-Fifty*. Enamoured of gypsy violins and ostentatious slaves, the queen of Pigalle jealously preserved the décor imagined before the war by a fan of the ballets russes: dark vaults, thick golden colonnades, heavy tapestry conjure up an imaginary Russia, sumptuously barbarian.

The days when Farouk came to court one of the singers in Shéhérazade, two tables away from Marlène Dietrich and Rita Hayworth, are over. But Peter Sellers and people reminiscing the great Russian clubs can still be seen. The atmosphere in this cabaret has an authentic and mysterious charm. The violinists are not necessarily Russian, but they can make you believe they are. Nitza Kodalban, the cimbalom player, has really played for Rasputin; at 75 he is not afraid of sleepless nights.

The cooking is honestly Russian, but can become "international" for Americans who don't wish to feast on vodka and blinis (roughly 80 to 160 francs . . . according to your appetite for caviar, salmon and champagne.) You can also stop for a drink there (36 francs with service) if you want to hear "Dark Eyes" and "Boublichkis" all over again, in this beautiful cabaret that suffers somewhat from the neighborhood's downfall.

Le Tsarevitch. 1, rue des Colonels-Renard, 425-72-99.
Just like *l'Etoile de Moscou,* is part of the Paoli fief, but you won't meet there the Corsican emperor of Eastern nights. He prefers the darkness of rue Arsène-Houssaye. His wife was able to hire a good chef and excellent entertainers. All the night-owls who fell in love with the Russia of the grand dukes, know the unmatched Valia Dimitrievitch, a gypsy who has a highly flexible voice with the range of an opera singer, and her partner, a song and dance girl. Supper is 100 to 150 francs . . . and more (depending on the champagne) Refreshments start at 30 francs. (Closed on Monday)

OTHER EXOTIC CABARETS

La Cabana Rythm. 42, rue Fontaine, 874-16-58.
Is managed by a solid and courteous trumpet player from the *Martinique,* who scorns the neighborhood and does not intend

to become a part of it. A few pretty and shapely swarthy girls, who dance well too, may accept a drink offered by a bachelor who admires exotic charms. But you might come in with your wife, if she likes the cha-cha, meringue and rumba. The orchestra is excellent.

For 30 or 35 francs they offer a spicy dinner, calypso music and other entertainment. At the bar, a drink will cost you 17 F, service included, a bottle of champagne at least 95 francs (at the table). (Closed on Monday)

La Canne à Sucre. 4, rue Sainte-Beuve, 222-23-25.

Has its own star: Gérard la Viny, a talented author-composer and guitarist who performs every night créole-style.

After the show-dinner (50 francs—all included) you might try their West-Indian supper served till a very late hour. Spicy "boudin pimenté" (black pudding) and "crabe faci" (stuffed crab) native dishes and good punches to wash them down. You could also take just a drink for 12 francs, at the ground-level bar, and 25 F in the room. Pleasant program from the Isles, "dou-dou" ballet (African), limbo and a palm to palm dance, singers with soft tropical voices. You will brush up on your beguine and merengue... (Closed on Sunday)

Djazair. 27, rue le la Huchette, 033-96-97.

Is authentically oriental, even the great singer Oum Kolthoum—the Arab Piaf—comes in to applaud their show. For at least 50 francs, they serve on copper trays, but you may opt for a drink only (starts at 17 F). Infidels don't have to worry about abstaining from alcohol (as decreed by the Prophet).

Six musicians lined up on a platform play endless Arab melodies that would make you dream of veiled beauties... if the charm of the dancing or singing girls from all over the Fertile Crescent did not satisfy you already. (Closed on Monday)

Djuri. 6, rue des Canettes, 326-60-15.

Prepares Greek-Balkan specialties for 15 or 20 francs, but the maître de maison offers more than his stuffed peppers or chicken-paprika. Djuri Cortes who is endowed with a beautiful voice and could serve as an interpreter at the U.N., sings in Russian, Hungarian, Yiddish, Hebrew, Greek, Romanian and Spanish, which does not explain his welcoming clients in French (Until 2 a.m.). (Closed on Monday)

L'Olympe. 15, rue de la Grange-Batelière, 824-46-65.

Offers vine leaves and sirtaki for some 30 or 35 francs or a drink at the bar. At hours when they set the type at the nearby "l'Equipe," Dario Moreno exercises her Greek wearing one of her eggshell or strawberry colored costumes. The fleet-owner Onassis comes in once in a while. (Closed on Tuesday)

La Table du Mandarin. 8 rue de l'Echelle, 073-63-76.
Creates a "chinese mood" for a bumpkin clientele that has great fun electing the Honorary Mandarin. The house in gold an laquered red, serves a very honorable sino-vietnamese cuisine. A nice program is rendered vaguely oriental by the ravishing presence of Tiny Yong. Service is courteous, the stage small and the check about 50 F.

MOSTLY MUSICAL

"*Chanson*"/ *Jazz*

SUPPER-CLUBS

"Show suppers take after the restaurant, cabaret, music-hall and "théâtre de chansonnier" world. The songs and dishes are very French, and better than most Parisians, who are ashamed to be seen there with country bumpkins, assume. You can often hear stars of ten years ago—professional if not still successful —and singers who abandoned the left bank style night club. They sing with enough self-assurance to make the audience "who hate to let the food get cold" interrupt their meal.

A few chansonniers dating from before the flood still make rhymes about the Général. It seems to amuse clients, but once in a while you are treated to stars like Gréco and Antoine.

Service can be fast so that by the time the singers go on, the "steack au poivre" (pepper steak) has been dished out. But too often can you still hear the crêpes-suzette crackling to a Brel tune (rarely sung by the composer). A member of the management regularly utters a loud "shh!" to quiet the clients who drown the verses with their conversation. It is hard to reconcile song and gastronomy even when the chef is good and the program well-done.

The blame usually falls less on the owners as on the diners, who sometimes show very little respect for the artist on stage. Yet the owners are the least caring in all of night time Paris:

high costs and unpredictable attendance often lead them into a deficit even if their cabaret is packed during holiday or Salon periods.

L'Acapulco. 107, rue de l'Université, corner rue Fabert, 468-91-96 and 97.

Has a loyal clientele of physicians, pharmacists and magistrates who work hard and like to laugh. They do so when Bouboule, the jack of all trades says to Gaby, "I'm gonna eat yours ears up." They laugh again when Yo-Yo the flower-girl sings, they laugh when a "miss" is elected and laugh some more when Gaby, the indefatiquable Basque, says or does anything.

Gaby who is good at his job, and Bouboule who is married to a Savoyarde know that the simplest formulas are often the best. At l'Acapulco, broad jokes and "gauloiseries" (joyous tales) are a way of life. Even the most reticent client ends up being caught up by the mood.

Service stops at 12:30 when the whole room, galvanized by Gaby, joins in old Boul' Mich Songs. The personnel sings along, the "vestiaire" (hat check girl) too . . . and you don't pay more than 30 or 35 francs, which is honest enough. At the bar, whiskey is 9 francs, service included. (Closed on Sunday and from July 10 to September 1)

Ma Cousine. 12, rue Norvins (place du Tertre), 606-49-35.

Is one of the last bastions on this lifeless and spiritless Butte-Montmartre. Abandoned by Jean Méjean, the emperor of night time Paris, this Montmartrian cabaret survives thanks to the rugged but lively Robert Rocca and singers such as Henri Gougaud or Henri Tachan who did not make the "hit parade" but know their material.

Show-suppers (60 francs minimum) until 1:30 a.m., refreshments from about 20 francs. (Closed on Thursday)

Le Don-Camilo / New Liberty's. 10, rue des Saints-Pères, 548-65-80.

After having been close to drowning, Jean Vergnes has finally reached dry land. *Don Camilo* became so successful that *le New-Liberty* later installed on the ground floor of the establishment doubled its popularity. Since he also owns *le Club des Saint-Pères* in the basement, Jean Vergnes now navigates a full ship in the Parisian night.

Many of his passengers are in the "cruise" age-group but can see a few youthful minettes cruising in and out the door, common to all three clubs. In the two supper clubs Vergnes features stars who have nothing yé-yé about them but who display a fine talent or vocal gift. You can hear there Robert Lamoureux, Henri Tissot, Roger Nicholas and Claude Nougaro, Pia Colombo or Cora Vaucaire. The program is plentiful and the prices reasonable. At the end of 1968, a dinner cost up to 148 francs —the latter including unlimited champagne (with apéritif and café of course). Non-diners have the right to a drink . . . when there is room. Vergnes does not stop expanding and yet he often has to turn people back.

La Grange au Bouc. 42, rue du Chevalier-de-la-Barre, 076-78-95.
Is managed by an old-time Montmartrian, lively and truculent. The kitchen doubles as a dressing room for the singers and strippers, the stage is only symbolic but the show keeps its pace with Rabelaisian fervor. To be precise, "le bouc" (billy goat) is none other than that tireless entertainer—the boss.

La Grignotière. 29, rue Mazarine, 033-81-58.
Is tiny, very crowded and fortunately air-conditioned. Right at the door you stumble upon a platform that serves as the stage. Robert Roccam Pauline Carton, Jean-Marie Proslier or Anne-Marie Carrière leave no play on words unturned but also give young and sometimes unknown performers a chance.

This small cabaret, serving late dinners, is regularly full to capacity. The program has variety, the food very fine and the prices are "tighter" than elsewhere: 62 francs for a dinner with wine, 84 F with champagne. You may order refreshments, 15 to 20 F . . . if there is some room left between the kitchen and the stage, when the diners are seated at the tables. (Closed on Sunday)

Le Lapin Agile. 4, rue des Saules, 606-85-87.
Is the Parthenon of Butte-Montmartre. Launched at the turn of the century by Bruant, frequented for a long time by Francis Carco, Pierre MacOrlan and other future academicians, it is today only a glorious vestige. Tourists still visit the place.

La Main au Panier. 3, rue de Poissy, 633-33-63.
Jack Authier, the Master of Ceremonies, is definitely less vulgar than the name of his establishment. After having told his funny stories and gags at Saint-Denis, Reunion, he returned to Paris where his success is now being promoted by out-of-towners (about 40 F).

Chez Patachou. 13, rue de Mont-Cenis, 606-30-46.
A few fragments of ties hanging from the ceiling are the only

reminders of the time when the little pastry-cook turned singer, had been scissor-happy. Patachou travels a lot and abandons her Montmartrian spot where Brassens and Feré and other celebrities then unknown would come by.

La Tete de l'Art. 5, avenue de l'Opéra, 073-64-4, and 53-39.

Was opened by Jean Méjean, then emperor of the Parisian night. When he had his financial waterloo, this establishment (as well as ma Cousine) was taken over by an industrialist named Pierre Guérin, but Robert Chauland, a discreet professional, stayed on as manager.

The show suppers are not given gratis, the check never descends below 120 francs (a drink is 46 francs, with service). But the prices are justified by the presence of stars never featured in other cabarets (Juliette Gréco, Roger Pierre and Jean Marc Thibault, Barbara or Nana Mouskouri).

As in the post-Belle-Epoque and unlike what goes on during most show supper today, the service here competes in politeness with the clientele . . . and the stars! The waiters work quietly, songs are not drowned by the rattle of dishes, and the customers forget to chat or chew during the acts, which is quite rare in cabarets.

La Villa d'Este. 4, rue Arsène-Houssaye, 359-78-44.

Belongs to M. Paoli, who apparently spends every one of his busy nights in his three establishments on rue Arsène-Houssaye. *La Villa* has a cabaret side. There idle young women gladly accept champagne from bachelors yet the entertainment is good and always features a star. Jacques Brel, who got his first pay check there came back, Colette Renard proved that she can be talented and libertine at the same time; Georges Chelon trained there immediately before appearing as a headliner at Bobino.

We don't have a special liking for M. Paoli, but he is reputed to be very fair (financially) to his artists—a behavior rare enough to warrant a special mention. To help him you can order the "menu-suggestion" for 40 F, but you may feel safe if you foresee 70 francs per person and even more if you like champagne.

THE "LEFT-BANK" CABARETS

In search of a stage even smaller than the one at the Olympia or Bobino we meet the cabarets called "left bank" (because there never were any similar ones on the right bank with the exception of the modest *Tire-Bouchon* in days bygone). They are very modest ante-chambers to Carnegie Hall and fame, but they were stepping stones for Jacques Brel and Barbara. They also help singers and other obscure artists (they do exist) express themselves or earn a living by "doubling" (see dictionary).

After "Amsterdam," Brel came back to sing for a pittance at *l'Echelle de Jacob,* because he had started there when he was still too timid to write "les Timides." From Trénet to Brassens and Aznavour, all the elders of "la chanson" sharpened their teeth in small cabarets where a drink costs little and an artist even less. Sometimes, they would walk home when they missed the last métro and could not afford a taxi, but they did gain experience.

The "yé-yé" revolution opened a new road to fame to the like of Jean-Philippe Smet who became Johnny Hallyday, skipping the left-bank cabaret stage. But the recorded voice only temporarily shook these places. For about two or three years, youngsters bought electric guitars on credit and thought they could all follow Sheila, the idol you never see on stage, but they were eventually disappointed. Together with record tycoons who saw their business drop, most of these would-be artists simply quit. A few bought regular guitars on their way back to the little cabaret where dreams sometimes become reality.

Le Caveau de la Boleé. 25, rue le l'Hirondelle, 326-59-15.
Serves cider to poor students and calvados (14 F) to tourists who love French obscenities sung by silver-toned voices. Since the foreign tabacco we use irritated the singers' vocal chords, we only heard a small part of their daring recital, but we can recommend it to amateurs of les Filles de la Rochelle (harbor girls).

Le Caveau de la Bolée, set up near place Saint-Michel in a beautiful cellar of a XIVth century abbey, was—so we are told—a nursery for very unhip young talent. We personally are totally insensitive to old French frolic, but we will believe it. (Closed on Sunday)

Le Cheval D'Or. 33, rue Descartes, 633-50-11.
Was layed out by the moustached M. Léon in an old habedashery. The decor has not been altered since the days of Suc and Serre.

Students and song lovers quietly listen with a drink (13 F) to singers like Ricet-Barrier (to be found all over the left bank and with great pleasure) or the fiery Petit Bobo whose stories smell of lavander and wild thyme. The show starts at about 11 p.m. It is well-paced, intelligent and often funny. (Closed on Monday)

L'Echelle de Jacob. 10, rue Jacob, 033-53-53.
Does not always star Brel, but it is being managed since recently by a friend of the composer of "Plat Pays." From 11 o'clock on, people come in hoards to the various levels of this cabaret to hear new talent (already polished) and professional entertainers. The program is eclectic and includes "non-singing" numbers such as one excellent bit by Myr and Myrovska. To enter the place you cross a gateway, then come into the joint through an inner door. Refreshments are 17 francs: a fair price if you can find a table. (Closed on Sunday)

L'Ecluse. 15, quai des Grands-Augustins.
Is a long hall with a stage where talented performers appear who can sing or make you laugh. People crowd silently to this little Olympia to hear promising young singers. Comfort is not its main attraction, but Barbara was discovered here. The program is quite varied: Avron and Evrard might follow Francesca Solleville. Drinks range from 10 to 24 francs (refills at 10 and 15 francs). The barmaid does not serve when a performer is on and goes as far as to unwillingly accept a tip while stating that service is included in the price. (Closed on Monday)

L'Ecole Buissonière. 10, rue de l'Arabalète, 707-25-81.
Has outlived the gentle René-Louis Lafforque, who created, loved and animated the place. You now find there Paul Preboist, a Southerner with an almost flegmatic sense of humour, Jean Harold, producer and narrator, and a few ladies who know how to adapt themselves to the Montmartrian spirit, such as Annie Fratellini or Suzanne Gabriello (who can do more than parodies). Dinner is served from 8 p.m. on for 50 francs, drinks are 15 F, service included.

La Galerie 55. 55, rue de Seine, 326-63-51.
Is more the territory of humorists than singers. Hubert Deschamps, Jacques Dufilho or Jacques Fabri had their début there thanks to the Parisian-Breton from la Gueltel, who demanded of his stars never to use low-keyed humor. A Colette Renard can put on a less bold program, but it would be rather stupid to admire only the display of Siné's drawings. The show starts at 11:30. Refreshments are 20 to 23 francs (a small "bar d'amis" on the lower level). (Closed on Sunday)

Chez Georges. (le Comptoir des Canettes) 11, rue des Canettes, 326-79-15.
Would be no more than a grocery-store that opens late (till 2 a.m. and used by well-informed Germanopratins) if it were not for its basement. Georges Chelon sang there before he ascended to the *Bobino,* Anne Vanderlove acquired a lot of experience there. The place is rustic but pleasant. (Closed when Georges decides)

La Méthode. corner rue Descarte—rue de la Montagne-Sainte-Geneviève, 033-22-43.
Does not have a methodical program. On certain hollow evenings the singers are as invisible as the clients. Though you may not find there regularly a Robert Nyel or a Romain Bouteille, you can always have a drink (sangria is 3.50 F) and stare at the old ceiling. You can also keep busy by listening to the long-haired clientele, young and rather nice, discussing the gastronomic charms of an eight-franc-steak and five-franc-moules marinière (mussels cooked with onions, spices and white wine). (Closed on Sunday)

Le Port du Salut. 163, bis, rue Saint-Jacques, 033-32-03.
Has left a fragile impression on those who had their portrait molded in plaster on the first floor, but the place is not without interest. You can find Bobby Lapointe, the interpreter of "Avanie et Framboise," there, also Maurice Fanon and the Abominable Pierre Doris. You may dine from 9 o'clock on, for 60 francs, the drinks are 15 and 18 francs at the table. (Closed on Monday)

Other song cabarets

—la Contrescarpe. place de la Contrescarpe, 633-44-64.
—la Vieille Grille. 1, rue du Puis-de-l'Ermite, 707-60-93.

JAZZ JOINTS

With a knowledge of classical music that runs from the first bars of Eine Kleine Nacht Musik to Beethoven's pom-pom-pom—pom, most French are relatively insensitive to jazz. They are right for the "bourrée" (Auvergnian dance) but not for bop—even if they believe they can jerk—yet they succeeded in putting aside the wholesome reading of Hughes Panassé and "La Rage de Vivre" to discover other clarinets. An intellectual but passionate minority follows Vian in his preference for the exciting music woven right in front of the public.

The quiet jazz fanatics are 30 to 40 years old and the younger set has been going back to it too. Curiously enough, they even reversed its evolution and started where their elders did, with the New-Orleans and going to free-jazz, passing through Count Basie, Duke Ellington, Charlie Parker and Stan Getz.

Black music that does not inspire clients to dance never seduced discotheque owners (sometimes at 4 a.m. when the place is almost empty they will venture to put on a good jazz record). In the present circumstances, we can recommend only *la Paillotte* (45, rue Monsieur-le-Prince) and especially *le Birdland* (corner rue Princesse and rue Guisarde) where Madeleine and Michel juggle rare records, after the closing of the *Storyville*. There you will meet musicians, escapees from *Castel* and chili con carne lovers (you can eat late, not too well, and pretty expensively).

If jazz is still listened to after midnight—and not only the Gaslight trio or Joe Turner (at *la Calavados*)—it is thanks to a few spots where they still appreciate a "boeuf" (see Dictionary) and where they pay musicians as well as they can because they like their music. The list is not very long:

L'Abbaye. 6 bis, rue de l'Abbaye, 033-27-77.
Intrigues the clients of *le King-Club* who go by the place on their way to a supper of exotic fish. Refreshments start at 9 F,

folk songs and negro-spirituals, a quiet and often foreign clientele. Neither discommended nor very highly recommended to jazz buffs. (Closed on Sunday)

Le Blue-Note. 27, rue d'artoirs, 225-18-92.
Was created in 1950 by Sugar Ray Robinson, the world champion in boxing, tapdancer, Parisian at heart and amateur of enlightened jazz. Until 1965, Ben Benjamin featired musicians like Lester Young, Kenny Clarke, Stan Getz, Bud Powell or Chet Baker, then the level dropped. Now this joint is only open periodically.

Le Caméléon. 57, rue Saint-André-des-Arts, 326-64-40.
Is directed by M. Pascal Fang, a Sino-Corsican as his name indicates. On the ground floor a moneyless long-haired clientele listens to good records. On the lower level, in a cellar too small to accomodate large groups, appear four or five musicians, sometimes French and good (like the Georges Arvanitas trio), and sometimes foreign and well-known such as Art Farmer or Slide Hampton.

The piano is falling apart but the welcome and general mood is warm. The long hair piling up in the basement is clean, a drink costs 8.50 F. in the discotheque and 18 F. in the cellar. (Closed on Tuesday)

Le Caveau de la Huchette. 5, rue de la Huchette, 326-65-05.
Has a different orchestra every night, but time seems to have irremediably been fixed in 1925. The older students who are discovering paleolithic jazz-à-la-française can bear the spartan hardness of the benches. You could not find much better for 7 francs, including cover charge.

Le Chat qui Pëche. 4, rue de la Huchette, 326-23-06.
Does free-jazz mewings. This is the joint where you can listen to Don Cherry or Marion Brown, the saxophone-friend of Ornette Coleman and Archie Shepp who only dreams of records and concerts. . . .

Living-jazz fans who did not arrest their development in middle-jazz loyally return to *le Chat qui Pêche* to hear the creative sounds of Armstrong and Béchet (15 francs cover charge, including a drink). Among them, few minets, no beatnicks but many musicians, come to hear their American collegues.

La Cigale. 124, bd Rochechouart, 606-59-29.
Some twelve years ago it brought together jazz lovers. It was not too good then and is much worse now. The mobile and

exotic clientele dances gracefully and asks no questions; a drink is at least 5 F.

Le Living Room. 25, rue du Colisée, 359-25-29.
Samson François, Milt Jackson, Oscar Peterson, Errol Garner as well as Chester Himes, the frenzied writer from Harlem, liked it. In an intimate and relaxed atmosphere, the fans of middle-jazz politely listen to the pianistics of Art Simmons and his little group that alternates with Aaron Bridgers, whose piano solos don't suspend the quiet chatter in the room. *Le Living Room,* managed by Joslin R. Bingham, otherwise known as Joss, does not close before 4 in the morning and frequently welcomes foreign musicians who can give a last minute "boeuf." 12 francs the drink. (Closed on Sunday)

Le Slow Club. 130, rue de Rivoli, 488-84-30.
Is better than its name. The clientele, very young, pays 7 francs during the week and 9 on Saturdays, which entitles them to entrance, a drink and good New Orleans groups. At the end of the week, Marc Leferrière plays a good old fashioned sax and the eternal Claude Lutet—who came to us from the mad nights of another Saint-Germain-des-Prés—plays on his clarinet tunes from the days when Béchet was discovered. (Closed on Monday)

Les Trois Mailletz. 56, rue Galande, 033-00-79.
Is set up comfortably in a very nice basement (a torture chamber with unusable sado-masochistic instruments on a still lower level). The joint, kept for the past twenty years by Mme Calvet, is forever denoted to mainstream jazz which we call "classical." 10 francs the shot (plus 2 F at the door); the customers are mostly in their forties; the musicians are French and foreign: Peanuts Holland, Bill Coleman, Don Byas, Memphis Slim. . . . (Closed on Monday)

This is practically all and it is not much. They also jazz it up at *le Riverboat* (67, rue Saint-André-des Arts) with good unknown performers. At *le Pub chez Félix* they have a few "boeufs" à la middle" sauce (23, rue Mouffetard). Nothing more, besides a few dawn improvisations at the *Bilboquet.* Young stars of the jerk and sometimes their directors—usually former musicians themselves—discover there a taste for swinging music called jazz.

SHOPPING

and Other Practical Information

LES DRUGSTORES

Le Drugstore des Champs-Elysées was inaugurated in 1958 in a zone where no night entrepreneur had ventured. After 8 p.m. the avenue was as dead as the unknown soldier. Ten years later, M. Bleustein-Blanchet's XXth century super-bazaar dominated the whole neighborhood with its discreet néon lights. A new breed of people, "les drugstorien," appeared there: insomniacs, loafers, buyers, some of them on the make, got into the habit of reading the paper there at 12:30, before shopping for after-shaving lotion, pocketbooks and records.

Within a few years, drugstoritis attacked Paris and contaminated the Western suburbs. A few cases have already been spotted in other provinces. In 1963, the promoters of the first drugstore launched *le Pub Renault,* curiously located behind the Alpines and R-16's in the back of an exhibition hall (since its shopping department is rather limited we mention it in the chapter on restaurants.)

In 1965, the team of Marcel-Bleustein-Blanchet started working on Saint-Germain-des-Prés, that old stronghold of the bohemian and intellectual way of life, that everybody believed immune to any American innovation. After mobilizing an army of experts and masons to dig their little labyrinth of mini-boutiques under an old building—with the help of Slavik, the decorator of the rediscovered "Belle Epoque"—they uplifted the face of the quartier without dissonance. Even M. Cazes, owner of *Lipp,* the club that symbolizes the perenniality of Saint-Germain can buy his paper here without losing face: an experience in successful (and peaceful) coexistence.

Imitators and adaptors hastened to create other islets of light for drifting nocturnes. Many of them called their variations names ending in "store" without seriously plagiarising the formula created in the Bleustein-Blanchet laboratories. The *Elysée-Store,* where stragglers would not stay long, had to be remodelled (reopening in Fall 1968). But the other establishments quickly acquired personalities of their own. *La Grande Maison de Blanc* was matched up with *le Drugstore Opéra,* a charming *Mini-Store* replaced *le Carnal,* that gigantic still-born cabaret where Jean Méjean had his Waterloo; *le Times-Square* found a home on avenue Victor-Hugo . . . in the dawn of 1968, *Berry 13* was born and *Armor's Store* discovered, while the baffling *Elysées-Bretagne* became successful.

Night-owls feel these innovations are satisfactory but still incomplete. Foreigners who explore the interesting but not too honest Parisian night feel reassured by the drugstores. There they meet autochtons who speak their language and menus printed in English, even fixed-prices and stabilizing ice-cream dishes to close a "frenglish" supper for 20 francs.

Le Drugstore Champs-Elysées. 133, Champs-Elysées, 225-94-90. Is the young daddy of all the "stores" in France and Navarre. There you find Guernesey pull-overs, hand knitted by the consciencious crochet-workers to the Royal Family of Great Britain, mustard with herbs from Meaux, lollypops as long as your arm, chinese vermicelli, all brands of cigarets, every newspaper, and 45 r.p.m. records. A remarkable library of pocket-books and novelties will allow you to catch up on your reading on quiet evening at home.

The pharmacy, first one in France to be integrated in such a complex, sells electric tooth brushes, acetylsalicilic acid in every form—even effervescent (the only true remedy for a hangover). It is also equipped to answer scientifically and deontologically for every microbial aggression.

Faithful drugstore customers don't necessarily dine in the part-nordic part-saloon paneled room. During popular hours the only thing to do is to stamp your foot by the closest table hoping to irritate the well-seated clients until they burn their finger in the coffee and decide to pay the check. Night-birds who come in at about midnight may be tempted by the seafood platters served there (the "géant" is superb for 36 francs) or by an enormous "club-sandwich" (6 F)—if they are alone.

Ice-cream sells better on Thursday, the young-set's day out, and on Sunday, the idler's day out (they are good consumers). But the minettes melt like a chocolate-sundae any time they see the fantastic portions as overflowing and colorful as in New York.

The "Vacherin" (sweet pastry with almond paste or meringue crown) kept a French name, but you will have to consult the menu for the exact contents of a Creol-Sunday and a Sweet-Sweet-Christiana. For the Sean Connery fans there is a Coupe-007 and if you choose the strange Coca-Cola-Float, don't feel you must sprinkle it with Cuba-Libre (a mixture of rum and cola, 3.80 F).

All this—and the Californian-Salad-Bowl—won't prevent you from eating French whenever a "boeuf gros-sel" (8 F) is featured!

In any case, this formula seems to be popular. More than 3,000 people visit the drugstores in one day, and the daily income reaches 7 million old francs. Few other businesses can boast such success!

Le New-Store.
Set up shop 70 numbers lower than *le Drugstore* without imitating it. Its flavor is quite different. You can often meet there "Paris-Match" people and young journalists of the Filipacchi group (the editing houses of "Salut les Copains" and "Mademoiselle Age Tendre" are very close by). The clientele is more Parisian, less mixed with tourists, than in other "stores."

Despite its "Los Angeles chicken" (8 F) and "Hawaiian steak with ham" (9 F) the cooking is honestly French. For 11 F you can order a roubust "carré d'agneau provençal" (loin of lamb with tomato and garlic), for less than 10 francs a "longe de veau" (top part of the loin of veal) or "potée savoyarde" (soup made of pork, vegetables and Gruyère). The salads are somewhat exotic; the chef at *le New-Store* is less pro-American than his collegue at *le Drugstore*. With a beautiful gesture of internationalism he created l'Egyptienne, la Chinoise and la salade Rio.

The bookstore at the *New-Store* does not always carry the latest contemporary intellectual works, but it offers serious reading at unbeatable soft-cover prices. The record and gadget shelves are well stocked. The latest Beatle record as well as Paco-Rabanne's toroise shell combs (50 francs) can be found there, the lumilite, an appliance that automatically recharges the electricity in an apartment has the disadvantage of costing 170 francs. A special mention to the poster department, if the fad has not died out by the time this guide comes out, and also the grocery managed by the efficient Edgar.

Le Drugstore Berri 13. 13, rue de Berri, 359-19-34.

Is not a haven for cooking as in Berry, but offers at all times good French food. Barely Americanized, it serves a fine "gigot" (leg of mutton) for 13 francs, "paupiettes de veau" (thin slices of veal, stuffed, rolled and braised), "boeuf gros-sel" (stock pot), and even "tripoux" (9 F). Good Châteauneuf-du-Pape: if you want a change from coke. . . .

Berrichons (from Berry) can dress Parisian style at le Berri 13 (suit: 380 francs. Jacket 150 francs), and they can also choose a pipe to smoke if they like Saint-Claude or Amsterdamer. The initiated are also familiar with the quality of the Sommer pipes. Heather or meerschaum from 15 to 715 francs.

L'Elysées-Bretagne. 4, avenue Franklin-Roosevelt, 359-20-63.

Is a very odd place. May foreigners in this store with a Breton flavor but a nordic setting. This complex (open till 2 a.m.) was still undergoing a few final touches when we were writing these lines, but its restaurant was already full to capacity.

The food as in Brittany is designed to feed husky fishermen. It is rustic yet delightful. *L'Elysées Bretagne,* the first resolutely regional drugstore, serves wheat crêpes and brown "galettes de sarrazin" (buck-wheat pancakes) at hours when all Douarnenez (in Bretagne) sleeps. You can discover there a good "cotriade" (fish dish): it is the Breton's bouillabaise.

A complete drugstore, this Breton embassy in Paris has a thriving food-shop. Basic groceries and main whiskeys are sold there and also "andouillettes" (small porc-sausages), cake à la bretonne and anything that can be washed down with Gros-Plan. Ouest-France and all the Breton newspapers are on sale at the bookstore, where apprentice-pilots of Vuarien can find, by the latest Sagan, maritime literature that smells of iodine. . . .

Le Time Square. 153, av. Victor-Hugo, 704-98-28.

Is just starting off in a section that usually sleeps by 10 o'clock: perfume and gadget boutiques open till 2 a.m. A restaurant (same management) gives the neighborhood's forlorn a chance to revive nearby.

Le Drugstore Opéra. 8, boulevard des Capucines, 073-08-60.

Was successfully implanted in a quartier where life stops when the chandelier in the Palais Garnier goes out. Strange movie people have created a bizarre menu where seafood platters are called Synopsis, Scénario and Panoramique (16 to 37 francs). This irritating menu is nonetheless honorable. It also features a good "fricandeau" (loin of veal: larded, braised or roasted) and "boeuf braisé" (braised beef) at a modest price (8.50 F).

For those who prefer to have supper for two at home, the grocery sells till 2 a.m. canned food, meat products, smoked fish and alcoholic beverages. If you wish to offer a mini-present to the mini-cook of your mini-supper, a "gadgetière" and "parfumerie" will make her forget that you did not stop by Cartier.

Of course it is much cheaper to buy a "série Noire" (mystery novel) and a 45 rpm record off the shelf and go home alone.

It would be unforgiveable to have photocopies or a key made at *le Drugstore-Opéra* without paying cash. While checkbook and Carte Bleue magnates cruelly close at 4:30 p.m., the little dynamic bank B.R.E.D. opens its windows from noon to midnight.

Le Mini-Drugstore le Madrid. 8, boulevard Montmartre, 824-97-22.
Competes with *l'Elysée Bretagne* despite its Iberian name. There you drown the appetizing buckwheat pancakes and sausages, eggs or ham with strong "cidre bouché" (high quality cider) imported from Tosporden. You will also find there "marennes" (oysters from Marennes) at 17.70 francs the dozen "moules" (mussels: 4.70 francs à la marinières), and the ritual "andouille de Guéméné" (pork sausages) till 1 a.m. The boulevardiers-on-a-spree go to bed earlier than their elysian counterparts. The cuisine is better than the composition of the menu where strange slogans stare back at you: "a vacation air: la paella, world famous Spanish speciality;" "unexpected: bébé-homard-Lucas (lobster). Our Forte." The turbot they served us there was sufficiently fresh to make any written comment like "the quality and preparation of our dishes have contributed to the success of le Madrid" superfluous.

The ocean-liner setting of this restaurant is pleasant. Upon your disembarking you can buy books, papers, cigarets and gadgets. For our little anecdote we will remind you that this little Drugstore occupies the quarters of *le Madrid,* a café more than a century old where Baudelaire versified and le Tour de France was thought up in 1902.

Le Drugstore Saint-Germain. 149, boulevard Saint-Germain. 548-42-63.
Makes better coffee than *les Deux Magots,* the tourist-oriented establishment across the street. In the drugstore tradition you will find here books, newspapers, cigarets, records and perfume.

As well as a pharmacy, entrenched behind a glass partition. The bearers of Mercury's wand, who can cure anything except drugstoritis, prefer to keep their distance.

The mesmerizing maze at *le Drugstore Saint-Germain* is not as complicated as the endless labyrinths of Borges, but you could almost lose your way between the bookstore (an authentic one) on the lower level and the restaurant on the first. During the popular hours of dinner, it is hard to find a table. But it is even harder to dine well in Saint-Germain-des-Prés for 20 francs, which is the average price charged in the Bleustein-Blanchet germanopratin fief. The relatively modest prices are even more remarkable if we remember that they spent 2 billion old francs just to set up the place.

Le Drug-West / Champs-Elysées. corner Champs-Elysées—rue Quentin-Bauchart, 225-74-92.

The latest elysian "store" was launched at the end of 1968 by the "Société française des drugstores" that had its start at Parly II and Elysée II. Specialising in real estate promotion, Robert de Balkany's group now concentrates its forces upon "les bazars de l'an 2000" (bazaars in the year 2000).

The former *Elysées-store* was taken apart by the architects of the three-leveled *Drug-West:* "snob snack," tobacco, books and shops on the ground level, restaurants on the mezzanine and first floor. Obedient children may order a special meal and big babies can munch till 2 a.m. on Texan hamburgers (very spicy) or beef with soy sauce followed by a strange "tarte pyjama." Estimate 25 francs for a playful dinner.

SHOPPING

Besides the drugstores, you may be interested in the following stores:

FOOD

—l'An 2000. 82, bld des Batignoles, 387-24-67.
A realgrocery, quality products, till 1 a.m.
—Charcuterie du Tertre (pork-butcher). 4. rue du Mont-Cenis. 076-72-63.

Open till 1 a.m., until 5 a.m. on Saturdays.
—la Cheval Vert. 25, rue Descartes, 633-50-11.
A restaurant (see appropriate chapter) selling take-along wines.
—Gangneron. 26, bld de Clichy, 254-55-69.
Pork-butcher open till 4 a.m. except on Mondays.
—Chez Georges. 11, rue des Cannettes, 326-79-15.
"Left bank" style cabaret (see chapter under this heading) in the basement, modest grocery store on the ground floor.
—la Maison du Caviar. 1, rue Vernet, 225-72-68.
Caviar, salmon, vodka, until 1 a.m.
—Mouff 5. 5, rue Mouffetard, 033-97-33.
Grocery for broke students, restaurant (see chapter under this heading) for comfortable beatnicks.
—la Quetsch. 6, rue des Capudines, 073-09-91.
Restaurant (see this chapter) and grocery, until 2 a.m.
—Tutti-Frutti. 7, rue Geoffroy-Marie.
Ordinary grocery, till 1 a.m.

FLOWERS

—Madame Renée. 47, rue Fontaine, 744-73-65.
Open for business (and deliveries) until midnight.

Books: Bookstores recommended by the very serious paper "le Monde;" open till midnight at least:

—bourrelier. 101, boulevard Montparnasse.
—librairie Continentale. 3, rue de Castiglione.
—Gallimard. 37, rue Bonaparte.
—la Hune. 179, bld Saint-Germain.
—la Joie de Lire (Maspero). 30, rue Saint-Severin.
—Yves Margotat. 8, rue de l'Odéon.
—Mattei. 40 boulevard de Clichy.
—la Pochade. 134, boulevard Saint-Germain.
—Trianon. 84, bld Rochechouart.
—Shakespeare. 37, rue de la Bûcherie.
—Saint-Germain-des-Prés. 184, boulevard Saint-Germain.

Tobacco: A few tobacco shops stay open late:
—le Balto (until 2 a.m.). 27, rue Victor-Macé, 878-53-04.
—la Belle Polonaise (2 a.m.). 21, rue de la Gaîté, 326-68-50.
—Bouquet St-Germain (all night, PMU betting). 16 rue du Four, 326-03-61.
—Fontania (all night, PMU). 25, rue Fontaine, 874-21-97.
—la Havane (2 a.m.). 4, place Clichy, 874-67-56.
—Mère Catherine (2 a.m.). place du Tertre.
—le Nid d'Aigle (all night). 22, rue Montorgueil, 508-45-03.
—Old Navy (2 a.m.). 150 bld St-Germain, 326-88-09.

A Nighttime Guide to Paris

—le Pigalle (2 a.m.). 22, bld de Clichy, 606-72-90.
—Raspail Vert (2 a.m.). 232, Bld Raspail. 033-64-52.
—Saint-Michel (4 a.m.). 10, place St. Michel, 633-08-08.
—le Tournon (5 a.m.). 8, rue de Tournon, 326-16-16.

Practical Information

EMERGENCIES

Accidents and disasters: In every case, it is best to call Police-Secours at number 17. They take care of everything especially if there is a need to summon the fire department, ambulance service, physician, hospital, etc.

Physicians: In very serious cases, when hospitalization is required, call Police-Secours, Otherwise call Docteur-Nuit at SOS 77-77. Two doctors connected to this central number by radio, circulate in Paris all night. They can arrive within the hour (50 F).

Pharmacies:
—Pharmacie Proniewski. 5, place Blanche, 874-77-99. Open all night, all week.
—Pharmacie Première. 24, boulveard Sébastopol, 887-62-30.
Open all night, except from Sunday to Monday.
—Pharmacies des Drug-stores. (see chapter on drug-stores)
Open until 2 a.m.

Centre antipoison (i.e. anti-suicide center): Call 205-63-29 any night, all week.

Hospitals, ambulances: Hospitals in Paris specialize in particular ailments: Cochin is for burns, Tenon for maternity etc. Here too Police-Secours is your best bet. In emergencies they will be able to call an ambulance service, request a motorcycle escort ("motards") and alert the hospital.

Car service: To reach a car or tow service for any car, call CEN. 10-00. 30 francs down ("forfait") + T.V.A (local tax)! Open all night.

Shopping   131

Household repairs: In case of a disaster (see above) the following numbers are useless. On the other hand, they are appropiate for small repairs: locks, plumbing, electricity etc.
—SOS 99-99. 25F down + 10 francs per 15 minutes additional.
—RIC. 00-13. 20 F. down + 20 F per hour additional (+ T.V.A.).

TRANSPORTATION

Car rental: One single company—Hertz. 27, rue Saint-Ferdinand, 425-99-69. Stays open till midnight.

Taxi: Call one of the following numbers:—ALE. 94-00, BOL. 77-77, PRL.-22-22, JUS. 67-89, PYR. 36-50, RIC. 28-30

Métro and bus:—last métros leaving between 12:30 and 12:45; arriving between 1:00 and 1:15 a.m.
—night buses. 13 lines. All leaving from Châtelet (avenue Victoria). Going toward every porte de Paris and back. Departures from Châtelet: every hour between 1:30 and 5:30. Returning every hour between 1:00 and 5:00.

COMMUNICATIONS

Information: We mention it full of enthusiasm. The girls at number 12 are as pleasant and efficient at night as they are disagreable and incompetent during the day. Ask them anything: telephone numbers of clubs, restaurants, cabarets. Dial 12 for a talking nighttime guide to Paris.

Wake-up service: dial 13.

Post offices: For all-night telephone and wire service:—8, place de la Bourse, 488-16-62.
—103, rue de Grenelle, 468-21-40.

APPENDIX
WHO'S WHO
AND DICTIONARY

Other Nocturnal Distractions

DANCES

The rascals on rue de Lappe are part of the prehistory of nightlife. But on quiet nights, tourists too dance the java at the Bastille. Apparently visitors know the *Petit Balcon's* sparkling better than Parisian, but the Balajo maintains its legend. Despite the Saturday night jerk, the accordion is still king under the starry ceiling of this large hall where the everyday Frenchman peacefully meets the little tourist who is exploring the fixed-price night.

There are other dances where the elegance of Tergal and Nylon predominate, but youth with its long hair rejects bagpipe music even when adapted. Don't bring that beautiful soubrette you intend to seduce. She has heard of discotheques and visits *le Bal de la Marine* or *le Mimi Pinson* only with her cousin in the service.

Here are a few addresses. Without comments. Do excuse us: we don't specialize in "dancings".
—Balajo. 9, rue de Lappe, 700-07-87.
—la Marine. 71, quai de Grenelle, 532-77-31.
—la Coupole. 102, bld Montparnasse, 326-95-90.
—l'Olympia. 28, bld des Capucines, 073-53-50.
—Mimi-Pinson. 79, av. des Champs-Elysées, 359-37-57.
—Royal Lieu. 2, rue des Italiens, 824-43-88.
—le Tahiti. 1, avenue de Clichy, 522-37-79.

GAMBLING

Here are a few addresses. No comments. Do forgive us: we prefer spending our money in other ways:
—Aviation-Club de France. 104, avenue de Champs-Elysées, 225-26-88.
—Billard Palace. 3, bld des Capucines, 075-48-80.
—Cercle Bonnes-Nouvelle. 206, bld Raspail, 033-96-11.
—Cercle Central des Lettres. 5, bld Montmartre, 488-18-02.
—Cercle Gaillon. 92, avenue des Champs-Elysées, 225-08-33.
—Cercle Haussmann. 22, rue de la Michodiére, 742-67-82.
—Cercle de l' Industrie. 2, rue de la Chausée —d'Antin, 824-91-40.
—le Grand Cercle. 12, rue de Presbourg, 533-30-60.
—Nouveau Cercle des Capucines. 6, bld des Capucines, 073-62-80.
—Opera-Club. 38, av. de l'Opéra, 073-87-31.

ELECTRICAL GAMES

Le Bowling. Jardin d'acclimatation (bois de Boulogne) 722-07-07.
Was set up in 1960 by Paul Pacini on territory borrowed from the monkeys and wild beasts and belonging to the City of Paris. After having sampled the 12 alleys (14 were under construction when this guide was being printed) and even piloted the "mini-racers" you can sit in the pleasant and sober setting of the quiet restaurant. Hot dinners are served till 11 p.m. only (25 to 35 F), but you can satisfy a sportsman's hunger with cold plates and sandwiches till 2 a.m.

You must pay the cerberus at the Jardin d'Acclimatation one franc for the right to wear bowling shoes and roll the ball at the pins (4 francs per game of 10 frames). Drinks are 4 to 10 F. There is a popular clientele on Sundays, a young and hip one on Thursdays and Saturdays. An air of peacefulness hovers over this scrupulously kept *Bowling*. On calm evenings when the weather is nice you can experience a feeling of the unreal there. The best of Pacini's creations after his *Whiskey à Gogo*.

OTHER DISTRACTIONS

Night cinemas:—les Trois Luxembourg. 67, rue Monsieur-le-Prince, 633-97-77.
Special midnight showing every day, in each of the three superposed mini-halls. Be careful, night features are different from the ones shown during the day.

"*Private Nights*"

The provincial coming out of the Débutantes, their ball and curtsies, and a few sad gala evenings given by a few charitable baronnes, makes one wonder about the grand Parisian night and the wit of a Tout-Paris that would probably bore Mme de Guermantes. But thanks to the megalomania of yankee producers and show-business VIP's, Parisians still buy Balenciaga dresses and await full of excitement these exclusive soirées. Fatuous or fiery parties are rare, but they would be nonexistant if not for the need of movie magnate to put themselves on show.

It is foreigners like Darryl Zanuck or Otto Preminger who threw the last sumptuous parties in Paris. Aside from Eddie Barclay, Pierre-Louis Guérin and the Frères Clerico (*le Lido*), Frenchmen no longer crave for fireworks and panache. They are the Père-Goriots of the Parisian night, spreading a few grains of caviar over dry bread when they must. They will invite their friends to an over-crowded cocktail party in clubs that charge them low prices. Because they are forced to fight over the bubbly offered at these "soirées," fashionable night owls anxiously await an opportunity to spend a distinguished evening in some place other than their favorite club.

★ A sumptuous Première at *le Lido* once every 24 months, featuring the Blue Bells totally nude and La Callas very much dressed up. Also present Bernard Buffet and Annabel, Liz Taylor on the arm of a robust Welshman, Michèle Morgan and Gérard Oury, practically every important American passing through Europe and all the French stars who know how to use fork and knife.

★ A crazy ball, somewhat "cheap" but droll enough to amuse Mary Quant, the Duke of Bedford and Suzy Volterra. Eddie Barclay has not been as turned on about parties ever since he took a wife and hired a manager with an accountant's soul. But the impresario of Brel, Dalida and Aznavour seems to be the only record magnate still capable of extravagances. He has had Tout-Paris glide on a toboggan, covered the Pavillon d'Armenovill with snow on a snow-less day, and shot fireworks from under the surface of a small lake in the Bois de Boulogne.

★ One or two grand film-evenings organized by Georges Cravenne, the man who had Piaf sing on the Eiffel Tower at the première of "The Longest Day" and Tino Rossi at the Opera on the occasion of "The Cardinal." These are the most beautiful gala evenings in Paris but they unfortunately depend on the more or less pro-French mood of American producers. Unless seized by a stroke of madness, Frenchmen are usually intimidated by Cravenne's parties. A big surprise, always expected but rarely occuring, will shake night owls into ordering a new tuxedo if not a full dress suit. We advise girls to wait for an invitation before rushing to Balmain, or Saint-Laurent, unless they want to refrsh their wardrobe for the two-supper evenings given each year at *Maxim's*. Eighty eminent Parisians gather around one theatre directress. . . .

All this would not be worth printing in this guidebook if not for the fact that six persons usually try to get in to these balls with one invitation. George Cravenne is not speaking terms with half of Paris because he cannot fit two people into a single chair. Risking to cause him more trouble, we will reveal to you that he classified Tout-Paris in a confidential file: applying his wordly sense of discrimination, he wrote down on blue cards those who will always be invited, while the unstable names appear on white sheets which a pitiless secretary can take out of circulation to make room for risking newcomers.

With his 12 regular associates and his temporary assistants, Cravenne periodically tries to beat the problem of squaring the circle of his worldly acquaintances. Tens of thousands of complaints from "indispensible" individuals have made him a philosopher. He now states that stars usually confuse the date and don't respond to their invitation, while some politicians discreetly excuse themselves . . . and ask that their cabinet head be invited instead.

Nighttime Who's Who

Bernardin, Alain has already sold razor blades, manufactured unsaleable boots, bought and resold old furniture and created *le Crazy Horse Saloon* in 1952. Husband and father, he designs the frames of his eye-glasses, his cuffs and the g-strings of his strippers.

He creates the acts and picks stage names with a taste for the absurd. (Rita Cadillac, Kiki Omnibus, Cora Lazzuli, Bertha von Paraboum). Intrigued by geography, he rolled the globe before launching Dodo d'Hambourg, Cha Londres, Consuelo Sao Paolo, Gora di Venezia and Victoria Nankin.

He smokes only Romeo and Juliettes ever since the *Crazy* expanded, buys only bargain cars (he found a convertible Volvo) and sleeps at Marly-le-Roi in a room hung with ticking, loves British humor, clicks his heels the German way and spends his vacation at Cadaque.

Casanova, Maurice. A moustached European-Algerian who monopolized one whole sidewalk of rue Saint-Benoît. He created *le Bilboquet* in the former premises of *la Discotheque* and *Club Saint-Germain,* then bought *l'Aquavit* which became *le Bistingo.*

He also owns *la Brocherie.*
He is associated with another bewhiskered fellow, Roland Pazzo di Borgo and has many other friends with subnasal growths, including Moustache.

Despite the young age of most of his customers (many idols and a lot of fans) he always has some twenty-five old "paroissiens" (see dictionary) who plays cards, sometimes "bilboquet" (cup-and-ball) and "jacquet" (backgammon).

Castel, Jean. Ex-student of HEC and inventor of an insecticide. He is without a doubt the most disinterested of night businessmen despite his commercial training. Under his management *l'Epi Club* was for many years the craziest and most wide-awake night spot in Paris, but it eventually sank, at the same time as his marriage. Jean Castel was managing *l'Epi* with Lotte—whose friendship he still cultivates and whom he visits in her club *le Black Jack*.

Jean Castel, who loves sailing, owns a sloop where the Deffe brothers turn ship's-boys for the Sainte-Maxime to Bonifaccio route. Regular customers on rue Princesse (where Castel now reigns over a discotheque, a restaurant, a bazaar and a pub), Sacha Distel's collaborators and public-relations men for C.B.S. records all trust this captain of the night implicitly.

Except for the time he takes off to travel to southern Corsica on seafaring vacations, and for the time he had to stay at the hospital (a result of his passion for fast cars), Castel is his own best customer. But he does not venture into the dark-rococco cavern where youngsters swing, preferring to stroll on the ground level between the bazaar, managed by Marc Doelnitz, César's bar, his "gang's" table and the booth of Huguette, the door-woman.

Farry, André. He spends his afternoons near Versailles, chasing after a golf ball but he has never yet left Montparnasse by night. A passionate collector of medals and trophies, a husband and father, he is the absolute ruler over the *O.K. bar,* and *la Villa* (connecting), *La Dolce Vita* and *le Black Jack,* now a discotheque. Golf and night living does not prevent him from managing his champagne business and a fashion-house. His apartment and offices are located right in the center of his Montparnasse territory, where he has been living for the past 20 years.

Francois-Patrice. Do not omit the hyphen in his name. He is very sensitive about it especially since his surname, Privat-Audouard de Saint-Hilaire, was somehow lost in the night. He is a comedian and has appeared in several films including "Escadron Blanc" and "Le Grand Rendez-vous," before becoming a night-owl at la Tortue (he recently went back to do "Les Yeux Cernés" produced by his client-friend, Robert Hossein) He had launched *la Licorne,* which is now *le Play-Boy* then crossed rue de Ponthieu to create *le Club Saint-Hilaire* in the hall of the *Carroll's* that was abandoned by Frède and the "garçonnes".

For six sleepless years, he was not able to come to terms with M. Sicre, the proprietor of the building, about the necessary renovations. So he emigrated to the left bank where he set up a *Nouveau Saint-Hilaire* in collaboration with Gérard Perrault.

In the summer, this unrepenting noctambulist spends his vacation at the *Saint-Hilaire-de-la-Mer,* in Saint-Maxime: he left night life only long enough to tend to a few ribs, broken in a car accident.

He has a wife, Colette, the only person to whom he has confessed his myopia.

Guérin, Pierre-Louis. No relations to the Guérin of *la Tête de l'Art*. He is the director of *le Lido* and a big exporter of French shows. His position is not only administrative—it is he who creates every two years the most famous superspectacle in Paris ... and organizes with Georges Cravenne, the only big Première with a cabaret setting.

A sensible man, he regularly goes out of the city to a sumptuous "moulin" (windmill) near Mauperthuis, Brie.

Guérin, Pierre. He is a businessman, known to hosiers, for whom he manufactures needles, in his factories at Laigle, in the department of Orne.

Although he was once the proprietor of *Montana,* a well-known bar in Montparnasse, he did not truly enter Parisian night-life until he bought part of the *A.B.C. club* and took over Jean Méjean's little crumbling empire. Pierre Guérin owns *la Téte de l'Art* and *Ma Cousine* and also manages his needle factories. A national advisor on international trade, he still finds time to watch over *Pacra*.

Marcel ("Monsieur Marcel"). One of the most discreet persons in the Parisian night, called by personnel, friends and collegues alike—respectfully—by his first name. Calm and wisely married, he placidly controls an unbelievable little world of transvestites, lesbians and strip-teasers. He created *Madame Arthur* and *le Carrousel* (which moved from the Champs-Elysées to Montparnasse) and "invented" shows featuring transvestites in an era when a sexual change created by hormones was still very limited.

No. 1 boss of Coccinelle, Bambi, Fétiche and other stars of acquired femininity, he also employs at the *Elle et Lui* ladies who take themselves for gentlemen. He personally supervises his cabarets (except the *Kit-Kat,* entrusted to the management of the sagacious Renou-Fradel), but gives a free hand to his friends, Gaby and Leila, who take care of *l'Acapulco-Tagada* and *le Ruby's Club.*

From his new office on rue Vavin, he coordinates the tours of the Carrousel show: they have already performed around the world, except for the U.S.S.R. and the U.S.A.

Martini, Hélène is queen at night, but she traded her crown for a collection of hats. She also succeeded in expanding her husband's empire. In Pigalle, her territory encompasses *les Folies-Pigalle (with her sister Alice as manager), le Pigalle's, le Sphynx* —that was being remodeled at the time we were writing this book—*le Narcisse, le Fifty-Fifty* and Sheherazade. On the Champs-Elysées, she is particularly fond of her *Raspoutine,* and lets Jean Well manage *le Pussy-Cat.* She also owns *l'Aiglon,* that may fall victim of a project to extend rue de Ponthieu, and le Batclan, one of the best known cabarets in Geneva.

She takes off once in a while for a rest in her country manor, but otherwise she is known for keeping late hours together with her associates, collegues and employees. Which does not prevent her from dabbling in the theatre world. Hélène Martini is the owner of the Bouffes-Parisiens and la Comédie de Paris.

Minski, Albert and Maxime. The Minski brothers work as twins, but you can tell them apart by their hair. While Maxime shaves indiscriminately, Albert prides himself in his moustache and lets his curly hair caress his neck. Maxime is an accountant at heart and spends his time in the discotheque—*King.* Albert on the other hand is the family promoter. He prefers to hang about the two floors where he set up two restaurants, a bar and a game for which he shows a definite weakness, billiards.

In love with the *King Club* which he created when he was still new to night-time society, Albert was first to emphasize comfort, luxuriousness and service. When night-financiers were meagerly supporting a trade that was supposed to take care of itself, he created the first American-style "night complex" and with this new formula took his place among the front-runners in night club business.

He was able to include his two hobbies—billiards and exotic fish —in his professional life, but he did not succeed in building an artificial ski slope on rue de l'Echaudé. This near-champion of "schuss" spends the month of February in Courchevel or Crans-sur-Seine (ski resorts).

Pacini, Paul. The unsteadiness of the too vast Miniland does not eliminate him from the history of Paris by night. This creator of the *Whiskey à Gogo* joints invented with Jean-Claude Merle the discotheque.

As he was playing the guitar and telling stores at *le Plancher des Vaches,* at l'Alpe-Huez, he discovered that just as much noise could be produced—and at lesser cost—with records instead of an orchestra. He then discovered a way to play more records per needle without damaging the 78 r.p.m. records and thought up a way to "personalize" whiskey bottles (which clients had been keeping under lock in their absence). He built a *Whiskey à Gogo* on rue de Beaujolais, on rue Marboeuf and in Cannes, set up *le Bowling* in the Bois de Boulogne, and launched le *Club de l'Etoile* under Potel and Chabot.

This quiet southerner loves April-fool jokes and gadgets, so he stocked up on toothpaste with whiskey and work-less watches. He also put scotch-in-ampoules on the market, under the name of Gogotine.

Paoli, Jacques. He is a very busy Corsican who divides his night between *la Villa d'Este, la Caravell* and *l'Etoile de Moscou*, on a 50 meter spread of rue Arsène-Houssaye. His wife heads *le Tsarevitch*. Napoleon's great-grand-children have forgotten his retreats from Russia.

Perrault, Gilles and Gérard. These are not brothers. Gilles is a lady, married to Gérard. The two owners of the *Sexy* separate at night. While Gilles supervises the cabaret and its batallion of pretty girls (she takes care of the show), Gérard turns into a pseudo-client at *le Nouveau Saint-Hilaire* He joined François-Patrice in expanding and remodeling the old *Elephant Blanc*, that had been abandoned by Jean Fradel.

Mme. Perrault, a quiet and reserved woman, never understood how her husband broke the bed in Patrice's Sainte-Maxime villa —after an all-night drive, this never-tiring man came down (like a ton of bricks) on the bed offered him by his future associate.

Régine. Mme Zubelberg, of Polish ancestry, was born in Brussels. She forfeited her hard to pronounce last name and imposed her given name in nocturnal circles and later in show-business.

A true performer, she lives right above *le New Jimmy's* (her suppers are very much sought after) and entertains Françoise Sagan, Serge Gainsbourg and Jean Cau . . . who in return tailor songs they write for her voice. Even the sensible Barbara felt Régine's magnetism when she nicknamed her "Gueule de Nuit:" "I am a night mouse, I come, I go, I go on . . . I am not daylight's love lips, I am from Montparnasse . . ." Régine, who had a sauna installed in her apartment though she hates to diet, sings the second stanza with conviction: " . . . God made me round, round; but it bothers me not, after all we can't turn our fate around."

The new star at the Pathé-Marconi did lose weight for her first and triumphant Musicorama (she had the jitters), but it is not to her figure that friends and enemies refer when they hail her "the strongest."

Vergnes, Jean. hides behind dark glasses his somewhat timid nature and an obsession for "complex establishments:" against wind and tide (and little understanding from his co-proprietor) this reformed gambler retained a flair for double or nothing and succeeded in building a discotheque (*les Saint-Pères*) a night restaurant, cabaret with show-supper. He is an absent-minded dreamer and an obstinate entrepreneur. He has long retained his mania of hiring all the available entertainers on place de Paris, as well as strange but harmless "Maîtres-Jacque" whose dolce vita he financed. Much more reasonable about it now, he is still friendly, discreet and effervescent. He will never fulfill his endless need to expand in every direction.

Dictionary

A

air (conditionnement d') A technique foreign to Frenchmen, who mostly use odd machinery that barely draws in tobacco smoke only to hurl it back full force on the smokers.

alcoolisme is a plague for solitary drinkers only. At 25, the editor of this guide book can, even when full of schnaps, proof-read manuscripts. Don't worry about distinguished public drinking, if you don't sit down on a client's chihuahua, nobody will bother you as long as you pay. Only the poor are called drunkards. In the event you collapse, the waiter will cajole you delicately and send you home in a taxi. But if you wish to stay sober, just have half a bottle of Postillon 10 proof with your dinner and systematically avoid drinking in clubs, pretending that you just came to watch.

amant de coeur Lover. A kept woman's luxury. He shares her bed but not the rent. The romantic lover sulks in night clubs on evenings his mistress entertains the paying gentleman, but he does not get a cut. Young "debutantes" will take a romantic lover when they fall in love or feel lonely, but then they dismiss him or pass him on to a girl friend.

amazone. A prostitute who had to take to the car in order to scour avenue George-V, the Champs-Elysées and the section around Porte Maillot, more efficiently. All may happen right in the car, but don't count on your "conquest" to save you a taxi trip home.

anglomanie. The avengers of Jeanne d'Arc are powerless against the Beatles, the Rolling Stones, posters and Carnaby street. France is preventing Britons from entering the Common Market, but it dedicates its fashions, a good part of its music and night-life to them.

The Pub has become a Parisian institution where beer is fresher than in London and where even hayseeds drink their whiskey on the rocks. At Castel's *Bedford Arm's* you can tarry till late, at *Pub Winston,* the *Grand Pub* and *London Tavern,* you may have a British dinner or supper. Good for lovers of old scotch and Cambridge sausages . . . even tea (not at *Castel's*).

This anglomania may seem very young, but as early as during the Belle Epoque, Parisians saw *Maxime* change its name to *Maxim's!*

art. Includes song and dance, but don't confuse it with pure art when you see the word in an English ad such as: "the only art house in Paris." In England and America, the word art often denotes nudity.

as (à l'). When a waiter brings a drink "à l'as," he does not consider his client a genius. The expression simply designates the No. 1 table.

aube. Dawn. Night people live upside down and go to bed when the sun and honest workers rise. When starting off in night-life they brag about coming home through the first traffic jams, but they soon sing another tune. Tired and intoxicated they can only think about having to wake up shortly. Too bad for the lively minis—they sleep till mid-afternoon—who are stuck with these insomniacs.

Many late stragglers in Saint-Germain-des-Prés and l'Etoile swear with drunken conviction that they will reform in the morning. Reassured by long winter nights that make them feel that they go to sleep at normal hours, these insomniacs are easily depressed by early and pale summer dawns.

B

---

bar. English word . . . derived from the French "barre" (rod). It is the one you lean on when you get hit by the price.

biquet. No longer used. See "minet."

boeuf. Enjoyed at the approaches of dawn, if you like jazz. These are jam sessions of collective improvisation organized on the spot by musicians.

bombe (faire la) Debauch. An expression best left to proponents of drinking bouts, banquet feasts and other such celebrations.

bombe (faire sauter à la). To bomb. (outmoded). In the days when everybody was playing with plastic explosives a joker would once in a while drop some home-made gadget in a nightclub dust-bin (politely, after closing hours). At least three discotheques lost their facades this way.

Boulogne (bois de). 900 hectars of ill-reputed greenery, from sundown to sun-up, ever since grown-ups got into the habit of playing there after the children had left. Open-air depravity seekers venturing in this park must have a liking for danger. Specialized police dogs add the chase to "Opération pudeur" which complements the regular control (motorised beat, trap-cars, bicycle cops, plain-clothes-men).

During daylight hours, the police advise you strongly against riot-causing nature games. At night they positively forbid them. Cars may not park, and pedestrians may not walk there between 10 p.m. and 5 a.m. in the summer, 8 p.m. to 6 a.m. in winter.

The park is no longer a place of perdition, but it still maintains some of its former charms. Now that the automotive craze has taken hold of prostitutes, only some twenty street-walkers wait under the foliage, while their sisters smartly speed along Porte Maillot. Homosexuals, found everywhere, are taking over the Bois. In 100 arrests, 30 are homosexuals, mostly transvestites.

Exhibitionists are fading away for want of watchers. Some still believe they have something to show, but your chances of meeting one of them are less than those of being caught speeding in a radar-controlled area. A speeding ticket in the Bois de Boulogne is good for at least 200 francs.

brigade. The personnel serving in restaurants. An establishment open from breakfast to late supper must employ a day "brigade" and a night "brigade:" this is why many restaurants, though very Parisian, refuse to receive customers after 11 p.m.

C

---

cabaret. This word is derived from the Netherlandish "cabret," which in turn originates in the French word "cambret" (little room). And this must be why the cabaret is only one step away from the bedroom.

cadeau (petit) "Little present." Disregard the adjective. It means the payment you make to a lady of the night.

cahier de police. In every cabaret, the names, ages and addresses of the personnel employed on the floor and on stage must be kept up to date in a book (usually with photographs). The police can come in to check it whenever they wish, though files on the hired workers are regularly sent to the Mondaine (see under 'M')

cave (faire la) Take inventory. An inspection done under the supervision of the boss, the cashier or the manager, to ascertain what is left in stock after the last client has left.

car When a cabaret owner awaits a "car," he is about to gorge the tourists with bubbly. When he calls the "car," the cops arrive.

cendrier. Ashtray. Serves as a receptacle for cigaret butts when you are tired of putting them out on the carpet. When a "cendrier" smokes, discreetly pour some of your neighbor's drink on it, after he has left for the dance floor.

chandelle. "Candle." Is easy to light, since it denotes a prostitute who waits standing up to be layed down.

cigare. Despite the progress made in nocturnal ventilation, it is better to smoke a cigar than to smell it. Offer long cigarillos to young women who think they are Lola Montes.

cigarettes. Buy some at the corner tabacco store if you don't want to pay through the nose in clubs. The young ladies you meet there smoke a lot and never carry any. They almost invariably go for the filter-tipped "blondes."

Don't bring too many to a cabaret. The B-girls collaborate with the cigaret-girls and will not accept your favorite brand.

clandés are clandestine brothels. Doormen and even the prudish author of this text could inform you as to their locations. They are officially known as hotels. Things were less confusing before Marthe Richard.

clientele. European-Algerians are noisy, minets are broke, stars think they can do anything, journalists never pay, manufacturers are vulgar, whores are degrading, homosexuals annoying, musicians shameless, Germans are heavy set, Americans are badly dressed, Italians are on the make, Lebanese look suspicious, editors are out of it, and businessmen are always tired. You alone, dear reader, are the ideal customer, that is if you aren't reading this guide book in prison.

The charm of a club is created by a well-proportioned clientele rather than by its decor. It must include very beautiful girls, a few distinguished ladies, two or three celebrities and anonymous tycoons who spend the money on which merry-makers and super-jerkers can be invited.

Clientele proportioning affects only those discotheques that have customers to choose from, others will welcome anybody. Cabaret owners never bother about the appearance of its customers; a "poussah" (fatso) wearing a maroon shirt and violet tie can open a bottle as proficiently as any gentleman dressed by the "Group des Cinq." We are far removed from the era of *Monseigneur, Florence* and *Carroll's,* when a few royal clients shaped the beautiful Parisian nights.

club (privé) is legal in France. A 1901 law governs non-profit associations such as *le Jockey*. Profit-oriented discotheques may not be considered private clubs and must open their doors to one and all. We don't suggest you come to a fashionable club with a policeman and legally force your way in. You won't feel at ease. . . .

cocktail. Except for a few bars in big hotels and at *Harry's*, most of the places carry the eternal Américano, the Whiskey-sour and Ginn-fizz only. At the *King-Club* you can fortunately sip through long straws "tropical" mixes and ask the barman on the first floor to mix you any drink.

complet. To clientele it means that they have to turn back. To club personnel it designates a bottle with all the extras: glasses, ice, cola, Périer.

comptabilité. Bookkeeping. In clubs, it is usually two-fold, except when the place is watched or about to be sold. Tax inspectors don't have any illusions about it, and correct the situation from time to time.

When cashiers prefer not to tamper with the actual figures, they keep two sets of books simultaneously, and are prepared at all times to hide the papers containing the actual receipts. It is just like in school: sometimes they get caught. Then case they have to complete back payments that can run in the millions and sometimes pay a fine. Of course they then start all over again. A night spot that would declare its true income would be irremediably condemned to never seeing any profit. (see also "taxes")

condé. You can call the "condés" and make a "condé." This word signifies both the police and the tacit agreement you can reach with them. In exchange for information leading to the exposure of big racketeers, they close their eyes to certain less reprehensible activities.

contraventions. Summons. Night policemen are strangely finicky at 2 in the morning. Ever since summons-stamps were introduced, it has been impossible to ask club owners to fix them, which they once promised without shame.

To spare their clientele any discomfort, some doormen delicately remove the "papillons" (tickets) from the cars parked in front of their establishment and tear them up in little pieces.

cravate. Tie. Requested in vulgar places because it looks distinguished and sometimes in distinguished places to eliminate vulgar customers. If you are a good or well-known client, they will take your scarf for a tie. Otherwise, the hat-check-girl will give you one which you, of course, won't put on.

D

danses. The tango has survived in dance halls only; the cha-cha, in a few clubs; the jerk is everywhere, even at the Balajo. Living off the dance as well as off whiskey, discotheques fully exploit the new rhythms after they saw the twist crowd their dance floors in 1960-61.

Except for the Brazilian bossa-nova, the Tahitian tamouré, the

Greek sirtaki, the letkiss (a kind of Lap polka) and the fayot, new dances in these last eight years have all been derived from transformed, adapted and corrupted rock. There were group-exercises such as the madison and hully-gully, the more individual transes like the mashed patatoes, the monkey, the monkiss, the shake, the surf, and finally the jerk.

Now satiated, night owls have become more conservative in their delirium or just stick to the slows. The rhythms now promoted by record companies no longer move the people. We are expecting a revolution. . . .

débutantes. Young ladies at the extreme limit of virginity who have danced at an annual ball led by Jacques Chazot . . . Most look better in a mini-skirt than in their first long gown and date in groups, those big ninnies of good families. When you meet them again in Saint-Tropez, they no longer look like debutantes.

deux heures (du matin). 2 a.m. Closing hour if the place has not obtained a special permit. The cancellation of such permits penalizes certain misbehaviors by club and night-restaurant owners.

disquaire. Disc-jockey in night-clubs. Instead of an orchestra, he (or she) plays 45 r.p.m.'s geared make you swing or sway. A good club-disc-jockey has to guess from his corner the sound level on the floor and in the room and know how to sustain the music. In night clubs, a dead interval of 3 or 4 seconds could seem an eternity. Fashion now calls for long-haired male disc-jockeys. The preceding trend called for sound-engineers in short dresses. These girls had the advantage of being able to make a quick visit to the dance-floor during the two or three minutes of a song—time enough to demonstrate a new step—but they had the disadvantage of delighting the customers too much. In any case, it is hard to find a "disquaire" who can create an aural atmosphere. A series of jerks cut off too abruptly or a succession of endless slows is enough to break the mood in a club. A mood that changes with the evening, the day, the clientele.

disques. Discotheques rarely use 33 r.p.m. records (because of the blank that separates the songs), but gobble up 45's, sometimes ordered from Great Britain and sometimes offered by record producing houses to promote their new titles.

Besides a few slows and songs by French rock tenors, club owners are partial to Anglo-Saxon productions, which supposedly are more appropriate for dancing. When you hear a Trenet or Brassens song you can safely bet that the interpreter of that song is in the room.

double carte. In certain dishonest restaurant the menu they show you to justify the check you find too steep is not the one from which you ordered caviar for your delicious partner. The dishes are the same but the prices considerably higher.

doubler. An entertainer doubles when he appears in two joints.

dragueur. He aspires to recline in good company as he stands by the bar. The hip new man-on-the-make will no longer bow stupidly when he invites a girl to dance. He storms the dance floor and interposes himself between a few cute jerkers, hoping that one of them will be too tired after the Rolling Stones to resist him.

If you know the management have yourself properly introduced to the lady by the master of ceremonies or the barman. Get some information about the young lady—she might be lying in wait for paying suckers.

drogue. Everybody claims it does not exist, but a few joints had to close up because the sweet scent odor of marijuana was floating in the air.

Cigarets filled with hashish can be recognized by the fact that a stump is more expensive than an entire pack of American cigarets. You may refuse, if you are offered any, for you may be gyped and smoke eucalyptus instead.

droit (des pauvres) has become a show-tax and does not concern the needy in the least. This and the sum owners have to hand the SACEM (see under S) are hitting cabaret proprietor hard.

E

échotier. Columnist. can pay the bill in billings.

F

Fernet Branca
They say it has medicinal powers at the approach of dawn. The bitterness of this black alcoholic drink is really so strong that it can shake up the most unconscious of drunkards.

filles. Basic night ingredient in the most restricted clubs as well as in the most specialized cabarets.

fils (de famille). Not always authentic. Even semi-prostitutes are sometimes mistaken. The departure of their fake fils-à-papa between detectives tells them that the car was borrowed and the checkbook stolen.

It also happens that real sons prove their strong personalities by commiting petty larceny and getting caught. The night is not too good to young night-owls who see their name written on a whiskey bottle more often than on a diploma.

folle. Masculine noun. All is not lost when "she" operates nights at Saint-Germain and on lower Champs-Elysées.

G

Gay Paris. An expression invented by tourists who took a long time to catch on that they were being taken in. If Paris—favorable to those who never go to sleep—offers a thousand stimulations, the exploiters of pleasures-by-neon-light play on the credulity, naivete or stupidity of their clients. The flock of tourists dragged by guides from car to cabaret, may not deserve any Dom Pérignon. But the cohort of foreigners and out-of-towners, gorged with bubbly and bad strip-tease, must feel like quitting and not paying. Unfortunately, the 70 or 80 francs for guided tours through the Parisian night are payed in advance.

gigolo. An obsolete person in the era of the pill and the mini-skirt. Neglected by women who prefer the easy-going minets, he has fallen back on homosexuals—who usually pay well.

H

habit. Full dress. Only head-waiters and outmoded princes don't rent theirs. Will guarantee great comic success when you dance the jerk in it.

hotels. Beware of the Salon de l'Auto and a few large fairs. Except for specialized residences and corroded lovers' nests on Pigalle, many sympathetic hotels are "full." Sometimes the police come down full strength (200 temporary closings in the beginning of 1968).

Feel free to ask any doorman for the address of a hôtel where you can check in with a companion but without luggage. Pay in advance and don't occupy the room too long. The three stars (of this type) are often set up in former "closed houses." You won't find there anybody to assist or replace your partner, but the decor will remind you of times bygone.

I/J

---

incendie. When ignited, night clubs don't burn down like vulgar factories or le Bazar de la Charité, they quietly go up in smoke after closing hours. *Hi-Fi* beat all records by burning down more thoroughly than *le Play-Boy* in Cannes, yet they were very hot under the collar at *le Bistingo, la Grignotière, le Crazy* and *le Bougnat* in 1966-67. Candidates now know that the most efficient way of setting a cabaret on fire is to divert the flame of a "chalumeau" (Blow Torch) onto the stage curtains (as one of the workers found out at *le Crazy*). If one lacks the necessary material, one may put a few cigaret butts between two cushions, but this method fills the place with a strong burnt smell—which is quite bothersome.

It is harder to put people on fire. With a sudden impulse and a British cigaret (it burns at a higher temperature) you can find some consolation in delicately burning a hole in your date's new Chanel. If she yells, beg her pardon and she does not notice, smirk silently.

K/L

---

licence. Licentiousness would not help an owner to obtain a "licence." Licence IV permits the sale of alcoholic beverages. Licence II permits it only with food. Since no new licences are being created in the département de la Seine, night spot owners have to buy up one owned by an establishment in jeopardy, then get permission to transfer it to their own place. A licence is rarely confiscated but a club on rue du Beaujolais proved recently that it can happen.

To get around the law that forbids one man to own several licences, night trustees officially transfer the administration of the extra clubs.

locomotive. They are essentially discotheque fauna, whose only contact with cabarets is the strip-tease of the *Crazy Horse* and the premières at the *Lido*. When they leave Paris it is to go to Courcheval, Mégève, Val d'Isère and Saint-Mortiz in winter; Cannes, Deauville or Saint-Tropez in the summer.

Most of the locomotives pay for the gangs they drag along, and then charge it to some society: promotion costs, "business" drinks. Some women too, surround themselves with an ample escort, but the word locomotive is only feminine when used by the S.N.C.F. (railroad). The title is given only to contenders of the stronger sex.

Note that pessimistic columnists speak of the "last locomotives:" the race is supposedly disappearing now that marriage has entered the life of the twist-era-noctambulist.

lunettes (noires). Dark glasses. prevents the midnight sun from overwhelming night revellers.

M

---

main (à la). This expression used by waiters, does not denote anything unhealthy. It simply means a bottle of champagne served without glasses or extras, to a table that already has all the accessories.

main (courante). May be your hand running over your neighbor's knee, but it usually denotes the book kept by the cashier: the one he shows to the fisc.

mari. Do not believe that the gentleman designated as the "mari" of a prostitute, married her in front of a judge. He is merely her keeper. When the owner of a girlie-bar affirms that he prefers married women (easier to manage), he is not expounding on marital virtues.

micheton. A term used by ladies of the night, B-girls, pay-off girls or prostitutes, for a man who pays, keeps them and sometimes thinks he is in love.

minet. A very young man with a pretty face and arching hips who drinks little when the check is not payed by an older woman or attentive man. Whether meant as romantic lover, gigolo or mignon, the minet is not gross and dances well. He is polite to his elders and only occasionally dishonest. When capable of dreams and vague plans for the future, he sees himself as an actor or singer, but this occupies him less than the clothes he wears. Despite his terror of military service, a minet loves uniforms when they come from the salons of Mayfair, Cardin or Renoma.

miroir (sans tain). One-way mirror. You are not the only one to look in. Very useful at a discotheque door, to look the clients over, amusing in some places where you don't have to go. Couples playing Narcissistic games are not alone, someone else is usually watching their prowess too.

mise en place. The work of waiters who prepare the room in the hour preceding the first arrivals.

Mondaine. The quiet client sitting at the bar, of whom they say: "C'est la Mondaine" is not a mondain homosexual, but a policeman who reminds the demi-mondaines that they are not ladies of the world after all.

moquette Fabric which club owners prize very much and obstinately preserve up to the last scrap.

mythomanie. Don't always believe the future plans of your bar neighbor or the honesty of the call girl who is entrusting her life to you after having borrowed some money for her old mother. Don't be afraid to tell anything and more. After two in the morning, everybody daydreams.

N

---

nudisme. Sometimes at the end of an alcoholic night, fine people will undress, but the Mondaine does not like it. Before the personnel gets a chance to ask the nudists to put their clothes back on, one can notice that these strip-teases are improvised by men and women who are sure of their muscle or breasts.

Modesty goes hand in hand with physical imperfections except in the case of transvestites who love to exhibit their newly acquired advantages while only slightly hiding the ones they lost.

O

offert. A drink that gives pleasure only to the drinker. The waiters indicate it to the cashier by specifying "en croix" or "en faillite" In unclear cases they will discreetly ask the owner, "avec ou sans musique?" (paying or not?).

P

papa. (or "mon oncle" or "tonton" or "mon ami"). A gentleman who keeps a young woman. He pays for relations which have nothing incestuous about them.

Paroissien. He lived out his youth madly and sometimes intellectually near an abbey he never visited. Now in his forties, he makes room for the yéyé and new somnambulists, but still evokes the golden era of Saint-Germain-des-Prés, the days of the one-man orchestra, Boris Vian.

The night dregs were scattered by the twist flood and the discotheques, but the legend of this section is not due to the present clubs. There are four Saint-Germain-des-Prés outside Paris (in Dordogne, le Loiret, le Maine and le Tarn) but the whole world knows "la paroisse" where young people were developing their talents between *les Magots* and *le Tabou, le Flore* and *la Rose Rouge*. They are "Les Paroissiens" described in Jean Cau's novel and les "Vieux Gamins" evoked by Annabel.

Some have emerged and maintain obvious reasons for frequenting a neighborhood limited by Plon, Julliard and Gallimard, others have been submerged by life. The adventure had started more than twenty years ago. The day de Gaulle was leaving power and presenting the program of the R.P.F., an article in the "Samedi Soir" officially acknowledged existensialism by publishing a photograph of Vadim and Gréco. He was a comedian, and she was playing with Michel de Ré's company.

It is in Saint-Germain-des-Prés that Sartre gave "Rue de Blancs Manteaux" to a Gréco that had not had her nose fixed yet. It was at Saint-Germain too that Boris Vian, Daniel Gélin, Anne-Marie Cazalis, les Frères Jacques, Yves Robert, Anouk Aimée and Nico Papatakis (then married), Guillaume Hanoteau, les frères Prévert, Joseph Kosma, Jean-Claude Merle and Marc Doelnitz made the Rose Rouge bloom, favoured aphorisms and hummed "les feuilles mortes". There they listened to Ferré, Montand, Mouloudji, Salvador Lemarque and Catherine Sauvage between improvisations by Sydney Béchet and Claude Luter...

The neighborhood now has its *Drugstore,* its restaurants for deluxe-yéyés, its clubs. Those who created it sometimes feel expatriated, but when you have a literary soul, nostalgia is not disagreeable.

patrons (de boite) Club-owners. Try to stay in the background when they own a cabaret and attempt to become stars when they have a discotheque. Each is convinced that he has the best program, the most thriving business and the most Parisian clientele in the trade. They have these illusions for a long time. Constantly falling out with each other they hate to play customer in another one's club.

photos. The ones sold under the hat are not always as obscene as you might think. Beware of reproductions of paintings in the Louvre. Though some of these documents bear witness to the imagination of Parisian girls and the vigor of their partners.

The price—30 to 200 francs—varies according to the number of models and the originality of their activity.

Amateur photographers are offered, at times, the opportunity to operate first hand. It is more intimate but also more costly.

pointe. Strippers can do a "pointe" and be totally ignorant about the "pas de deux." We refer here to the hand sewn triangle they stick on with double-faced tape, there where the fig leaf should be.

portier. Baptised "voiturier" (car keeper) when he keeps watch in front of a discotheque with jaguarized clients, the doorman is a person who is not about to tip his hat for nothing. He is badly payed and must know how to park cars and use psychology. The tips given by lonely clients are more generous in the measure that the information they reward is confidential.

In front of most cabarets, doormen praise the charms of the girls inside, they each claim that theirs are the prettiest and the easiest too. In return these porters are paid "au bouchon," they get a cut for each bottle of champagne uncorked at the table of clients they hustled in.

portière. A female cerberus whose job it is to close the door of a club to undesirables, strangers and sometimes well-known persons she does not recognize. One does not just become portière overnight, it is a trade that requires a long apprenticeship in the night.

provinciaux. French speaking strangers.

racket. A somewhat outmoded occupation, regularly tried by young men with the ardor and accent of mediteraneans. The racket, despite courageous attempts, hardly touched discotheques. Extortionists prefer to attack bars and cabarets with which they are more familiar.

Racketeers prefer to leech on to former collegues, now settled down. Before stupidely wasting munitions, they gain entrance to the joint disguised as clients then send out feelers by refusing to pay. If the boss resists them, calls the police or has them thrown out by his gorillas, they usually leave for good. But if he gives in, the inoportune visitor will propose a verbal contract which the owner will find hard to break. After evaluating the owner's income, these racketeers will make him pay dearly for protection . . . against other racketeers.

Certain neighborhoods like Saint-Germain-des-Prés, have not been troubled by such hoods, the latter preferring to visit these places as customers, after their own business hours. On the other hand, in Pigalle they cannot be avoided—frankly it is impossible when owners welcome juveniles who are in the habit of pricing their love. Things can work out if the boss is related to some magistrate who knows how to set his own law or if he is known to be very chummy with the police. Most of all he has to know the game and play it well.

For honest neophytes, the best solution is not to show their fear . . . and not to be afraid to call the police. This may seem obvious, but policemen investigating into such rackets know that no witness is more irresolute and unclear than a club owner.

ristourne. percentage given to touts, taxi drivers, hotel-porter, and girls who send or bring clents to a certain cabaret, night restaurant or even "clandé."

This custom is totally ignored in discotheques and a few cabarets, but many establishments raise their prices tremendously. Taxi drivers may earn 60 francs or even more for rerouting a client to a certain uninteresting cabaret. We don't have to add that these cabarets owners finance these kickbacks at the expense of the clientele; they can't afford to take it out of their general overhead.

S

S.A.C.E.M. Société des Auteurs et Compositeurs de Musique, cursed by discotheque and carbaret bosses, take 8.25% of the money earned and redistributes it among the composers of strip-tunes. In certain cases, the SACEM may tolerate transgressions but it usually cannot be had.

The conductors in cabarets write down every tune they play, so the rights can be divided fairly (sharp-eared investigators pay regular anonymous visits to cabarets). Disc-jockeys cannot possibly write down every piece they play between 10 p.m. and dawn, so the SACEM bases its every piece on model-lists from a few discotheques.

salle (faire la). Does not refer to housework. This expression designates the work of songstresses, dancers and, mostly, strippers who cross the footlights and find themselves mingling with the clients who are interested in the charms they saw on stage.

These young ladies are always thirsty. At 4 or 5 a.m. the cashier hands them their envelopes. They are payed according to the refreshments they drank with solitary patrons.

serveur is richer than many of his customers . . . when he has many of them. Paid according to a system of points, he only gets a symbolic salary and is too proper to refuse tips.

Sometimes, waiters in discotheques call some of their customers by their first name. These are the ones they meet in other discotheques when they too are customers and the waiter there calls them by their first name.

siège. Bench. Customers complain about hard benches, but it seems that they fall asleep on comfortable ones. The problem in any case is not that important, thousands of clients have endured the *Crazy Horse* stools for ten years.

siphons Only the mini-siphons from *chez Castel* are used normally. Preferring to add Périer or cola to their whiskey, revelers generally use the siphons to sprinkle their neighbor joyfully. Don't take offense at it, just ask your waiter for a towel.

smoking. Tuxedo. Worn when "evening attire only" is specified. Any crazy set of clothing will do now that the Mao suit expanded the horizons of the "smoking."

sortie de secours. Emergency exit. The owner and the waiters know where it is located. In case of emergency just follow them.

staff. Reasonably priced material that can be shaped into into beautiful beams of marvellous old stones, but unfortunately sounds hollow when assaulted. In some cabarets, the word staff means the drink served to a B-girl (and bought by a customer) this drink consists of 99% cola and the rest is whiskey....

suicide. Dawn game played by starlets who feel hopeless early in the morning. They recover well from a suicide attempt with barbiturates and this incites them to try it again at hours when they are sure to bother some "saviour" who just wants to go to sleep. At their third abortive try they get married and quiet down for good. Call Police-Secours and write down the number of "centre anti-poision." An accident could always happen.

T

tables Low enough in clubs so customers can't roll under them, they can also be:

—too heavy. You will be trapped when you get up to dance.
—too narrow. You are bound to spill your drink.
—too closed in. You will spill your neighbor's drink.
—too cluttered. You will spill everything.

All this will be meaningless on days you won't find any.

taxes. Cabaret owners would be condemned to live like paupers from flourishing cabarets if they did not cheat a little in their bookkeeping and did not extract a few personal profits from general costs. The following is what the French nation gets from the flood of somnambulist-clubs: 21% on two thirds of their income, and 16.66% on the last third. Since the creation of the T.V.A. this imposition has replaced the 8.50% taxation on turnover and 12 or 15% show tax on the returns.

—5% on the salary of the personnel.
—400 francs of Social Security payed monthly for each declared employee.
—50 francs per employee allowance.
—70% or 50% on the profits if the business is owned by a single person or an organization.
Add to this the percentage taken by the SACEM for redistribution to the authors and composers of the music: it varies from 6.6% to 8.35% according to the fixedprice asked and the musical "sources" (orchestra or records).

taxi. Younger cabbies, somewhat less scheming than their elders, and new radio-taxis did not stop foreigners (naive or half-willing) from doing some strange tours of Paris when they let their driver decide for them.

Most of the drivers just do their job, though they know as much about night life as any policeman or vagrant, but others are in cahoots with very profitable "cabarets à ristourne." That little envelope brings in more than the mileage on their comptometer. Their passengers will undoubtedly drink to their health in cabarets to which the cabby sent them.

touristes. Regreting more having entered a cabaret than not having been able to enter a club.

treize. There is no table number thirteen in night joints. The fisc knows that the cashier is not trying to cheat them when he skips from Table No. 12 to table No. 14 in his records.

truqueurs. Fake homos who give in to real ones for money. Easily contacted on the lower part of the Champs Elysées, Pigalle and Saint-Germain des Prés, these young people sometimes have disquieting hobbies. They resort to theft and blackmail to make ends meet. The Mondaine writes the names of known truquereurs on blue cards, but has effective weapons against the criminals of homosexuality who can blend in a crowd of perfectly honest minets. Nor do many of their victims press charges....

V
---

vacances. Thousands of Frenchmen look for a change in scenery; you can make do with a just change in alcohol. Follow Régine to Deauville, Paul Pacini to Canne, François-Patrice to

Saint-Tropez and Leila to Biarritz . . . and buy an ultra-violet lamp.

vernis. The elegant varnish of Parisian night-owls does not always go as far as the wearing of nail-polish with a tuxedo.

verre. A drink or glass. May be drunk, broken, turned over, thrown, but in all cases: paid.

vestiaire. Assisted by the cold and bad weather, she fears good weather that drains her savings. In summer she makes a living from the sale of cigarets only.

The chief cloakroom attendant is queen in her little kingdom, which she may rent. She hires her assistants and pays them, watches the restrooms and the telephones. Besides her cigarets, she has sewing material and a mini-pharmacy (give her at least one franc per clothing item checked and don't try to escape under the pretense that you only have a large bill, she is perfectly able to give change.)

videur. Empties the clients who empty too many bottles. Can be recognized by quick reflexes and a slow mind. The last videurs have taken refuge in Pigalle. They are too anesthetic for discotheques. Sometimes an owner may ask the Mondaine to send a discreet inspector, or call upon a few tough friends and ask them to wear ties, to bash a few heads in.

zone (protégée) To prevent school children and senior citizens from gobbling up Dom Pérignon and Chivas, it is forbidden to create any night establishment that sells alcohol at tempting distance. No license can be obtained by clubs created within 50 meters from a school or 100 meters from a retirement home. The insane are least likely to spend many mad nights. They are surrounded by a protective zone of 200 meters.